GOD HAS SPOKEN

GOD HAS SPOKEN

BUT WHAT IS THE CONCISION?

LIONEL C BATKE

For my faithful sister Lauradel

ACKNOWLEDGMENTS

Many years ago, I had breakfast with my pastor Les Prichard. As we sat sipping coffee waiting for our eggs and bacon to be served, Les looked me full in the face and asked, 'Lionel, what is the Concision?'

I was speechless. Although my father was a pastor and I was a child of the church, I'd never heard of the Concision. Les proceeded to draw a Cross on his napkin and listed some 'old' things on the left and some 'new things' on the right. This simple but powerful principle, along with many others, grew into this book you are reading, a book which I believe can be used in any seminary or Bible School in North America or the whole world.

Years later, in 1978, during a Sunday morning service in Vancouver, the congregation gathered around to lay hands on me for my first mission trip to Ireland. During their prayers someone prophesied there would be a man in Ireland who would take me to the Catholics.

Thirteen years later I met Brendan McCauley at the Christian Renewal Centre in Rostrevor, Co. Down. I took Brendan to the nations and Brendan did indeed take me to the Catholics, all over Ireland and all over Slovakia.

Brendan also produced two books for me, this one and my first book, *The Key of Knowledge*.

When Pilate said to Jesus, 'What is truth?" he asked the wrong question. It's very hard to give a right answer if people insist on asking the wrong question.

Lionel Batke

CONTENTS

PROLOGUE

⧉

Written by Brendan McCauley

I'VE TRAVELLED with Lionel into many nations and have spent countless hours in his company. We've sheltered under banyan trees in the blistering heat of an Indian afternoon, eaten sockeye salmon in Alert Bay, BC, been attacked by ravenous belly button sucking leaches in Sri Lanka, eaten a hot dog in Indonesia, and supped ice-cold Guinness as we watched wild swans landing on the tranquil lakes of Killarney, Ireland. At least I supped Guinness, Lionel drank hot English tea.

Lionel and I have been described as chalk and cheese. Perhaps our friend the Indian apostle Thampy said it best, when he told hundreds of Indian pastors we were 'a good combination'.

Lionel with his gimlet eye deftly explaining deep biblical truths with a sharp spiritual scalpel that separates soul and spirit and I hang gliding with the Lord on the warm winds of dreams, visions, and prophecies. Lionel with both feet on the ground and me in mid-air. We both inhabit the prophetic realms though we rarely step on one another's toes.

I'm a storyteller, a man of a thousand books. Lionel is a teacher, a man of one book. Lionel labours long and hard and daily mines priceless treasure from his beloved volume. Often his teaching, preaching, prophesying, and conversation contain rare key insights that suddenly unlock doors into new hallways and rooms of revelation.

Such moments remind me of the proverb that says, A word fitly spoken is like apples of gold in settings of silver.[1] Perhaps a more appropriate version might be,

> Like apples of gold in settings of silver, so
> is a word skilfully spoken.[2]

Lionel's new book, *God Has Spoken*, is jam-packed with a lifetime's treasure of insight and revelation that has helped make Lionel one of Canada's most respected teachers of God's word at home and in the nations. Lionel is like the man Jesus affirmed,

> Every student of the Scriptures who

becomes a disciple in the kingdom of heaven is like someone who brings out new and old treasures from the storeroom.[3]

GOD HAS SPOKEN!

'In many separate revelations - each of
which set forth a portion of the Truth-
and in different ways God spoke of old
to our forefathers in and by the
prophets, but in these last days God has
spoken to us in His Son'.[1]

GOD HAS SPOKEN but who is listening? Is anyone
interested enough to 'pay much closer attention to the
truths we have heard'? (Heb 2:1 Amp) Then we are chal-
lenged with another question. Does anyone care enough
to 'seek (truth) as for silver and search as for hidden
treasure?' (Prv 2:4). This suggests nuggets of silver are
seldom found lying around on the surface. Seams of

silver and gold are usually discovered running through subterranean layers of granite.

On the surface they may appear unimportant and insignificant, but below ground they widen into a wealth of untold riches. The treasure trove of Truth we seek needs to be mined up from the depths of discovery. 'It is the glory of God to conceal a matter, but the glory of kings to search out a matter' (Prv 25:2). We 'kings and priests' (Rev 1:6) need to dig a little deeper!

These were things 'which at the first 'began to be spoken by the Lord and were confirmed to us by those who heard Him' (Heb 2:3). Everything God desires us to know about Himself and every other related subject, He revealed in the Bible. 'These things (were) written that you may know you have eternal life' (1 Jn 5:13) and mature as Christians (2 Tim 3:16,17).

'Whatever things were written, were written for our learning, that through patience and comfort of the Scriptures, we might have hope' (Rom 15:4). Again, we are told 'all these things were written for our admonition' (1 Cor 10:11) which is more than 'learning'. 'Admonition' is a pep talk to help us become 'holy' (1 Pet 1:16) and 'free' - 'you shall know the truth, and the truth shall make you free' (Jn 8:32).

The God of history revealed Himself and 'spoke to Moses face to face, as a man speaks to his friend' (Ex 33:11). That's when he saw how it all began, when Moses traced time back through Genesis until it disappeared into eternity past. 'The beginning' (Gen 1:1) of the world is expressly and deliberately indefinite, as is the end of the world.

The Lord said, 'I will put you in a cleft of the rock till my Majesty sweeps past you (Moffat), then I will remove my Hand and you shall see my afterglow (TWOT) facing West (Strong)' (Ex 33:22,23). When Moses came out of the cleft of the rock 'facing West' he saw where the 'Sun of Righteousness' (Mal 4:2) had been, having disappeared over the horizon but leaving behind the most glorious - indescribable and stunning sunset this world or even 'the world that then was' (2 Pet 3:6) - has ever seen. And this was just the 'afterglow'!

REGENERATION

'What man knows the things of man
except the spirit of man which is in
him? Even so no one knows the things
of God except the Spirit of God...the
natural, nonspiritual man does not
accept, welcome or admit into his heart
the gifts, teachings and revelations of
the Spirit of God, for they are folly
(meaningless nonsense to him), and he
is incapable of knowing - of progressively recognizing, understanding and
becoming better acquainted with them
- because they are spiritually discerned,
estimated and appreciated'.[1]

THE 'NATURAL MAN' cannot understand the Scriptures. Man without the Holy Spirit can no more understand the 'things of God' than a monkey can understand the 'things of man'. A monkey does not understand how a car works and could never fix it, much less design and build it. That's not because he doesn't have a brain and a body. It's because he doesn't have the 'spirit of man' in him.

God never breathed into a monkey's nostrils or any other member of the animal kingdom. 'The Lord formed man of the dust of the earth and breathed into his nostrils the breath of life' (Gen 2:7). God is truly the 'father of spirits' (Heb 12:9) individually, and Father of the 'spirit of man' corporately. God's own breath is in man! God's breath and the 'spirit of man' in you, is the one and **only** difference between monkeys and men!

The Jewish 'rulers did not know Christ nor even the voices of the Prophets which (they) read every Sabbath' (Act 13:27) because the unregenerate mind or 'natural man' is incapable of understanding the Scriptures.

HERMEN WHO?

'HERMENEUTICS' is an Anglicized form of the Greek word 'hermeneuo' meaning 'to interpret, explain in words, expound' (Thayer[1], Kittel[2]). Hermeneutics also comes from a cognate used when Jesus 'beginning at Moses and all the prophets, He expounded to them in all the Scriptures the things concerning Himself' (Lk 24:27).

This word means 'to thoroughly explain, expound, interpret and unfold the meaning of what is said' (Strong[3], Thayer). In order to do this, He had to give a correct understanding of the historical context before interpreting and applying a given passage to Himself in that day. Hermeneutics may be defined therefore, as the science of rightly understanding and correctly interpreting and applying the Scriptures.

11

Why is God's language misunderstood? The difficulty is not with God's manner of speaking. The difficulty is with the dullness of our human understanding. We who are bound by time and materialism, are slow to grasp things that are spiritual and eternal. 'Peter said to (Jesus), Explain this parable to us and He said, 'Are you also even yet dull and ignorant - without understanding and unable to put things together?' (Mat 15:15,16 Amp).

God used specific kinds of language to communicate His thoughts to us. This is particularly true when He speaks through the prophets and says 'I will open my mouth in a parable, I will utter dark sayings' (Psa 78:2). Failure to recognize this has led to numerous and conflicting interpretations. God's choice of words is clearly seen in the Scriptures.

Israel had their beginnings at Mt Horeb (Ex 33:6) where Elijah returned 400 years later for a fresh start (1 Kgs 19:8). This 'mount of God' called Horeb is where 'the pillar of cloud descended and stood at the door of...his (Moses' own personal) tent (Ex 33:7) and the Lord talked with Moses' (33:9).

How did He do that? What manner of speech did God use when He 'talked with Moses'? Did He speak plainly?

Did He mean what He said and say what He meant? Does He mean what He says and say what He means today? How are we to know if He says one thing and means another?

Later on in the desert, again 'the Lord came down in the pillar of cloud...and He said, If there is a prophet among you, I the Lord, make Myself known to him in a vision, I speak to him in a dream. But not so with Moses...with him, I speak face to face, even clearly, plainly and apparently and not in dark speeches' (Num 12:5-8 AMP,NKJ,KJV). So the books of Moses are written in flat, doctrinal, historical, plain language.

God said many times He would speak 'plainly'. This 'plainly apparent' manner of speaking can be called 'literal' speech - that is, 'according to the letter, not figurative or metaphorical'. God uses this language in the Pentateuch and other historical records, including the Gospels and epistles. This kind of language does not need to be interpreted. It needs to be taken at face value, in terms of the plain sense in which it is given, and just believed - not interpreted.

However, God also plainly said when He spoke through the prophets he would use another kind of speech. The

Scriptures of the prophets abound with parables, symbols and figures of speech. If the truth is to be discovered and known, these things need to be rightly understood and correctly interpreted.

There are two ways in which the same word for revelation is used in Scripture. Revelation comes through the written Word because 'secret things belong to our God, but those things which are revealed (galah) belong to us, that we may practice all the words of this law' (Deu 29:29 NBV).

The Holy Spirit also brings direct revelation to people because 'the Lord does nothing unless He reveals (galah) His secret to His prophets' (Ams 3:7) - so revelation comes by both the Spirit and the Word.

THE LAMPLIGHTER

'HOW DO YOU READ...WHAT is written?' (Lk 10:26) When
Jesus asked this question, the 'lawyer' (Lk 10:25,29) gave
a right answer but the wrong interpretation, because he
insisted on reading the Scripture his way. He missed it
by wilfully twisting the text. That we read the Word of
God is not nearly so important as 'how' we read it.

We must learn to read the Bible God's way!

Jesus also said, 'Take heed therefore how you hear' (Lk
8:18). That we hear from God is not nearly so important
as 'how' we hear what God is saying. Eight times John
says in Revelation, 'he that has an ear, let him hear'. Ten
times Jesus says in the Gospels, 'he that has ears to hear,
let him hear'.

We must learn to hear from God His way. This warning is preceded with, 'No one when he has lit a lamp covers it...but sets it on a lampstand, that those who enter may see the light. For nothing is secret that will not be revealed, nor hidden that will not be known and come to light' (Lk 8:16,17 NKJ).

'Your Word is a lamp unto my feet, and a light unto my path' (Psa 119:105 NKJ). You need to decide how much light you want. Some only want enough light for their 'feet'. Others want enough to light up their 'path' and pierce the darkness far ahead - 800 yards down the road!

> 'Your future lies before you
> Like newly fallen snow
> Be careful how you tread it
> For every step will show' (Anon)

How we hold and 'handle the Word of God' (2 Cor 4:2) is crucial. If you hold the 'lamp' up front and centre, the light will blind you. If you hold it behind your back, you will walk in your own darkness. But if you hold the 'lamp' up and to one side, it will light up your path. The 'Word of God' must be carefully positioned so we can 'see the light'.

This is why both pulpit and bible are off to one side

in some traditional churches. They know the church is Christ-centred, not bible-centred. But the church must be bible-based. To be effective, the 'Word of God' must be given its proper place.

'Whatever God says is full of living power, it is sharper than the sharpest dagger, cutting swift and deep into our innermost thoughts and desires (LB) it can slip through the place where the soul is divided from the spirit (JB) exposing us for what we really are (LB)' (Heb 4:12).

Like Moses (Ex 4:10), King George VI stuttered and struggled to speak in public. In a broadcast at the end of 1939, just three months into World War II, the King said to the man who stood at the gate of the year, 'Give me a light, that I may tread safely into the unknown'. The man replied, 'Go out into the darkness and put your hand into the Hand of God. That shall be to you better than light, and safer than a known way'. This prophetic utterance given in weakness, has endured through the years.

'Who among you fears the Lord, who obeys the voice of His Servant? Look, all you who kindle a fire, who encircle yourselves with sparks. Walk in the light of your fire, in the sparks you have kindled - you shall lie down in torment' (Isa 50:10,11 NKJ).

We can 'kindle' our own sparks, or even generate and walk in our own light by disobeying 'His voice'. The key to walking in the light of God, is obedience. No wonder David cried 'Oh, send out Your light and your truth! Let them lead me, let them bring me...to Your tabernacle' (Psa 43:3).

SIGNS AND SIGNALS

SOLOMON SAID he wrote some things down to help us 'understand a proverb and a figure of speech or an enigma with its interpretation, the words of the wise and their dark sayings or riddles' (Prv 1:6 Amp). God Himself said the truth would be hidden in 'dark speeches' (Num 12:8), 'visions' and 'symbols' (Hos 12:10 NKJ) that do need to be interpreted.

Zechariah spoke of a 'woman sitting in a basket' trying to seduce all mankind in the commercial world (5:7). Then he said, 'two women' took the basket to Babylon where it was 'set there on its base' (5:9,10). The entire Babylonian basis and foundation for commercialism and humanism John says in Revelation, is doomed to sudden destruction at the end of the world, and it will be irrevocable.

Ezekiel spoke in 'riddles and parables' (17:2). The prophet spoke of wheels with eyes, an eagle, a cedar and a vine, sour grapes, a boiling pot, a valley of dry bones and a river of living water. Zechariah spoke of red speckled and white horses, myrtle trees, four carpenters, two olive trees and living water flowing from a cleft mountain.

Daniel spoke of a 'stone' that became a 'great mountain' (2:35), a horn that spoke (7:8), a ram and goat at war (8:5,6). Isaiah referred to trees clapping their hands, wells of salvation and valleys being exalted.

Jesus also used this kind of language when He said the Kingdom of God is like a sower, a mustard seed, a treasure in a field, a pearl of great price, a net full of fish, ten virgins with lamps and a wedding feast. He said men must 'eat His flesh and drink His blood' in order to have eternal life.

The book of Revelation is 'signified' (Rev 1:1) which means 'to communicate, indicate, intimate, mark by signs or signals, to have a deeper meaning, to represent' (Strong, Kittel, Weymouth). This word is used in different ways throughout the New Testament to describe powerful prophetic 'signs' and 'signals' that 'marked' their generation. Jesus said Jonah was a 'sign'. Isaiah said he and his children were 'signs and wonders from the Lord' (Isa 8:18).

When you read Revelation, it's not like reading the newspaper! This book is written in 'representative' speech. These amazing representations and colorful figures of speech must all be rightly understood and correctly interpreted before the truth can be known. In representative speech, the 'sign' or 'signal' must always mean the same thing. In traffic, a red light can never mean something else. In redemption, a dragon can never mean a savior.

John spoke of Israel as a 'great mountain, blazing with fire, thrown into the sea' that sank, sizzling into the depths (Rev 8:8). He saw millions of 'scorpions' pouring out of Hell like clouds of black 'smoke' billowing up into the heavens until the 'sun and the air were darkened' (9:2,3), 'locusts with faces like men, and hair like women' (9:7,8), a huge, fire breathing 'red dragon' thrashing the heavens with his tail, just waiting to murder the Man Child 'as soon as it was born' (12:3-5) - and another awful 'beast with ten horns rising up out of the sea' (13:1).

21

John saw the most enormous world colossus standing astride the whole earth 'with a rainbow (like a halo) over his head, his face (shining) like the sun, his right foot planted upon the sea and his left foot' in the middle of a continent, towering up into space. When He 'raised His right hand to heaven and swore…that time should be no more' - everything on earth came to a full stop (Rev 10:1,2,5,6 Amp).

KEYS TO INTERPRETATION

⧽

IN ALL AGES, godly men and scholars have differed in their opinions and conclusions as to what God intended to teach us in certain passages. As a result, there are many thousands of segregated denominations each camping around the revelation of some 'portion of the truth' (Heb 1:1 Amp).

We are all like 'fish' (Mat 4:19) spawned in some pool or great lake of local churches connected for the propagation of a particular emphasis. We grew up on a special diet of nutrients thinking we had the whole truth and nothing but the truth.

Then the great twentieth century Pentecostal and Charismatic outpouring of the Holy Spirit caused all the pools and lakes to overflow so a vast ocean was created where all fish can swim freely. We discovered there are rich nutrients of truth in all the pools and lakes.

However, not everyone is convinced. The unlearned critic blatantly ridicules and rejects the Bible as being 'full of impossible contradictions and absurd nonsense'. Others, who quote 'God said what He meant and meant what He said' as a solution to all difficulties, simply ignore their problems or they are ignorant of the extent of Scripture.

Does all this mean the Bible cannot be understood? Did God leave us in the dark to grope for truth and interpret Scripture based on our own thoughts and ideas? No, thank God there are clear guidelines and keys to correct interpretation.

INSPIRATION

'ALL SCRIPTURE IS GOD-BREATHED (AMP, or) given by inspiration' (2 Tim 3:16). When Nicodemus 'came to Jesus by night' and said You're a great 'Teacher' (Jn 3:2) he was wrong. Jesus is the great 'Breather' - the One who 'breathed the breath of life' into our nostrils, **and** into the Scriptures.

That doesn't mean 'all Scripture' is the Word of God! Some of it is the word of the Devil, and many others who did not speak the Word of God. However, I accept affirm and believe in the full and complete, word by word inspiration of the Bible, or accepted canon of Holy Scriptures which are thus infallible, true and correct in their original consensus of manuscripts and therefore, the supreme and final authority in all matters of faith and practice.

There were thousands of early manuscripts but 99+% of all technical problems have been solved in the last 150 years. This provides a solid and firm foundation on which to build 'the faith once and for all delivered to the saints' (Jud 3). The Almighty Creator communicated His thoughts, purposes and promises to His creatures by Words, and recorded them in a Book 'for our learning'.

Paul said that 'to the Jews, were committed the oracles of God' (Rom 3:1,2) which refer to the Old Testament. Stephen said 'This is that Moses...who was with the Angel who spoke to him on Mount Sinai, the one who received living oracles' (Act 7:38) - not dead legends. These 'living oracles of God' are truly, the best thing this world has to offer!

ILLUMINATION

YOU MAY BE A BELIEVER, but even believers do not
understand the Scriptures without illumination because
'the twelve (apostles)…understood nothing of these
things, His words were a mystery and hidden from them
and they did not comprehend what He was telling them'
(Lk 18:31,34 Amp).

Isaiah said 'the hearts of this people have grown dull,
their ears are hard of hearing and their eyes they have
closed lest they should see with their eyes and hear with
their ears…but blessed are your eyes for they see and
your ears for they hear, for many prophets desired to
see what you see and did not see it, and to hear what you
hear and did not hear it.' (Mat 13:15-17).

Paul said 'their minds were grown hard and calloused - they became dull and lost the power of understanding, for until this present day when the Old Testament is being read...Yes, down to this (very) day whenever Moses is read a veil lies on their hearts and minds. But whenever a person turns to the Lord the veil is stripped off and taken away' (2 Cor 3:14-16 Amp).

Some say the veil is taken away when you turn to the Lord personally and you're placed 'in Christ' but it's not taken away until you place Christ, not Moses, in the Old Testament text. If you read Moses into it, the veil is still there! So suspect the text. Suspect the text of what? Suspect the text is talking about Christ!

Some are 'ever learning and never able to come to the knowledge of the truth' (2 Tim 3:7) because they refuse to read Christ into the text. It's not because they cannot read or do not study, but because they do not properly interpret what they read.

The Holy Spirit was sent to 'guide (us) into all truth' (Jn 16:13), to 'teach (us) all things' (14:26) and 'open (our) understanding that (we) might comprehend the Scriptures' (Lk 24:45). This requires a close personal relationship or walk with God and the development of our spiritual 'senses' (Heb 5:14). Truth illuminated by the Holy Spirit is inspirational - warm and gripping.

SCOPE

SCOPE HAS to do with the over-all intention or purpose of the writer. There are seven 'sign' miracles John told us about in his Gospel. Then he said 'These are written that you may believe Jesus is the Christ, the Son of God' (Jn 20:31). All the lessons and miracles should therefore be viewed in the light of his stated purpose. This purpose governs our understanding of all he says in the book.

'No prophecy of Scripture is of any private interpretation' (1 Pet 1:20). The word 'private' is 'pertaining to one's own self' (Strong) that is 'separate' and 'apart' from the rest of Scripture. So to determine correct interpretation we need to take all the Scripture has to say on any given subject.

'The entrance and unfolding of Your Word gives light, it gives understanding and comprehension to the simple' (Psa 119:130 Amp). Truth that is more darkly represented in one verse or passage, is more clearly revealed in others. 'These things we speak not in words which man's wisdom teaches but which the Holy Spirit teaches, comparing spiritual things with spiritual' (1 Cor 3:13). Only by 'comparing' Scripture with Scripture can we come to a true and correct interpretation.

One verse or passage will unlock, open up and unpack another so they amazingly illustrate and support one another. When Christ was tempted in the desert for 'forty days' (Lk 4:2) the devil quoted Scripture. He repeatedly misapplied and misinterpreted the text.

Jesus said, 'It is written' again and again - leaving us an excellent example of 'comparing' Scripture with Scripture. This 'comparing' and compiling the sum of all Scripture is necessary before drawing a conclusion or attempting to form doctrine. Many Christians are not interested in 'doctrine'. They just want to be happy and go to Heaven, but the early apostles 'filled Jerusalem with doctrine' (Act 5:28).

CONTEXT

CONTEXT DENOTES A 'CONNECTION OF THOUGHT' and refers to revelation which precedes and follows the subject in order to properly understand the Scripture. In establishing doctrine by so called 'proof text' one must be careful not to seek support from an isolated or obscure verse taken out of context. A Scripture must not be taken out of its setting.

The true subject, time and place or geography must be discovered in order to correctly interpret the text. Failure to use due diligence in determining the true subject of a passage is probably responsible for more error in Bible interpretation than any other single cause. If God is speaking to or about a certain person or persons and we make it mean something else, we twist the truth and miss the message.

Many passages which belong to believers have been applied to unbelievers. A classic example is 'How shall we escape if we neglect so great a salvation?" (Heb 2:3). This is a warning to which few Christians take heed because it has so often been taken out of context and applied to unbelievers. Scripture can have an application to many persons or places and circumstances but must abide by the revealed subject of the passage.

There's always only one interpretation, but there can be many applications. A promise given to a named person can only have an application in principle, to others. Express commands to named individuals must not be taken as commands or promises to anyone else. After Abraham was commanded to sacrifice his son Isaac on the altar, and Jephthah decided to do the same thing it ended in disaster (Jgs 11:34,35).

What right then, do we have to claim the Great Commission to 'Go into all the world and preach the Gospel' (Mk 16:15)? The 'authority' we have to claim and obey this command in spite of great opposition and real, professional persecution comes from Christ himself. 'Jesus spoke' to His 'disciples' and said '**All** authority is given unto Me...Go and make (more) disciples of **all** nations' (Mat 28:16,18,19).

In some cases, the subject is not clearly defined and must be carefully sought out. In other cases, it may be stated metaphorically and need to be interpreted. The true subject can be discovered by careful examination of the Scriptural, historical and cultural context, by comparison with other parallel passages, by locating New Testament quotations of Old Testament statements and by observing safeguards for correct interpretation.

WORD MEANINGS

THE ENGLISH DICTIONARY is not the place to go when trying to determine the meaning of some Bible word. The true meaning must be discovered and determined from original Greek and Hebrew texts used to convey thought, and from the way the word is used. This can be done by using a concordance, lexicon, Greek and Hebrew commentaries and by comparing several translations.

Translators often give brilliant insight into the original meaning of words. Unfortunately, the true meaning of a word or phrase is sometimes covered over or even twisted and misrepresented due to their own personal bias, doctrinal predisposition or blindness to the truth. This can leave the casual reader with a wrong impression or lead to a completely misguided conclusion. For instance, 'The **meaning** of the language' should be and is translated 'the power (dunamis) of the sound' (1 Cor 14:11 Douay/Reims). 'Dunamis' is used 18 times in First and Second Corinthians and is translated 17 times with the usual word 'power'.

However, in this verse it's completely covered up! Why hide the word for 'power' with such a mild and weak word that hardly bears repeating? Paul is saying 'If I do not know the force and significance of the speech' (Amp) I can't communicate. He's saying, 'sounds' have 'power'!

Over time, words change and often lose their original meaning. For instance, the word 'meet' is a mystery until we learn the original word means 'fit' or we have been 'qualified to be partakers' (Col 1:12) through Christ. The word 'conversation' has changed to mean 'our citizenship is in heaven' (Php 3:20) so it's not what we say that's in heaven, but the registration, rights and privileges we have in belonging to that country.

Oriental customs, historical context and geography all have a bearing on rightly understanding and correctly interpreting Scripture. When we are told 'If your enemy is hungry, feed him...for in so doing you will heap coals of fire on his head' (Rom 12:20) we need to know they used to carry live coals in potsherds on their heads.

When your enemy's fire is out and his house is cold with no way to restart his fire, the hot coals you 'heap on his head' will surely warm his heart as well as his house. He knows he treated you badly. Now these passages glow with amazing revelation!

FOUNDATIONS

MOST DOCTRINES ARE REFERRED to in many different passages, but there is always one specific book or chapter that systematically sets forth a teaching in extensive detail. Doctrine should be formed from and based on these passages.

Study should proceed in an orderly manner beginning with these passages, then move to more difficult, isolated and obscure texts, fitting figures of speech into clear, plain statements that thereby interpret Scripture with Scripture. These difficult texts must always be understood and interpreted in the light of their foundational passage.

For instance, Romans is the only book in the Bible that systematically sets forth the doctrine of salvation, beginning in chapters 1 to 3. Galatians adds to this foundation. Justification before God is explained in Romans 4 and 5, justification before men in James 2. Water baptism is laid down in Romans 6 and baptism in the Holy Spirit in Acts 2.

Acts is without question, our foundation for studying the work of the Holy Spirit. This book is truly, the Acts of the Holy Spirit, not the acts of the apostles. Romans 12 and 1 Corinthians 12 to 14 are the foundation for spiritual gifts. The resurrection of Christ is established in chapter 15. Ephesians is the foundation for the people of God, Matthew 5 and 6 for the kingdom of God. The second coming of Christ is taught in 1 Thessalonians 4 and 5, also 2 Peter 3.

The Scripture says, 'Your commandment is exceedingly broad' (Psa 119:96 Amp) so God has given us an 'exceedingly broad' base or foundation on which to build truth. Isolated obscure and more difficult texts should then be fitted into the superstructure, being understood and interpreted in the light of clear teaching that is more detailed, extensive and explanatory.

'Behold, the Lord stood on a wall with a plumb line in His hand' (Ams 7:8). If a foundation is faulty or crooked and out of plumb, the higher we build on it the more out of line the whole structure becomes. When that happens people have two choices, either straighten the wall or kill the prophet. They have often done the latter, but if we are willing to do the hard work, reconstruct our position and straighten the wall it will be to our great benefit.

When teaching is built on a single verse or two it's like standing a triangle on its head. Doctrines made to stand on their head have to be propped up to keep from falling over. It is a great error to build doctrine on some obscure text or doubtful premise.

<u>The</u>
<u>obscure</u>
<u>isolated</u>
<u>more difficult</u>
<u>statements and</u>
<u>verses of Scripture</u>
<u>'line upon line'</u>
<u>'precept upon precept'</u>
<u>'exceedingly broad' base</u>

Isolated, difficult, hard to understand or ambiguous texts need to be built upon and interpreted in the light of this 'exceedingly broad' base. This foundation of flat, doctrinal language forms a straight and solid 'pillar and ground of truth' (1 Tim 3:15).

We have already learned that when God spoke through the prophets He used 'dark speeches', 'multiplied visions', 'symbols', dreams and riddles. Much of Jesus' teaching was in parables. All these things need careful interpretation.

However, the historic narratives, the life of Jesus and many others, their miracles and exploits are statements of fact recorded in plain, straightforward language. A large portion of Scripture is written in clear and simple statements of fact that do not require interpretation. They just need to be believed and obeyed!

DEFINITIONS

'SIMILITUDE' is an all-inclusive word that refers to rhetorical, abstract language like similes, symbols, metaphors, types, allegories and picturesque or representative speech. 'Figurative' language likewise refers to representative or symbolic speech.

A 'simile' is a figure of speech expressing similarity by using the words 'like unto' or 'as it were'. 'The street of the city was pure gold, **as it were** transparent glass' (Rev 21:21). 'The city was pure gold, **like unto** clear glass' (Rev 21:18).

A 'metaphor' is a stronger resemblance between two things, using something natural to describe a spiritual reality. Jesus said: 'I **am** the vine' (Jn 15:1), 'This **is** my body' (Mat 26:26) or 'Tell **that** old fox' (Lk 13:34). A simile says, 'God is **like** a rock' but a metaphor says, 'God **is** a rock', which is stronger.

Legitimate 'hyperbole' is an exaggeration not meant to be taken literally. 'May the Lord...make you a thousand times more numerous than you are and bless you as He has promised' (Deu 1:11). That prayer is intended to result in a population explosion that will astound the mind.

'Analogies' are associated words or things with similarity, likeness or resemblance. This is a process of reasoning by comparing cases that resemble each other in function, but not necessarily structure or position. White is analogous to purity (Dan 7:9), black is analogous to sin (Lam 4:6,8) and red is analogous to wrath (blood) or judgment.

An 'allegory' is an example, a factual story with a literal meaning but which also has an intended figurative, spiritual or moral lesson. 'Abraham had two sons...which things are an allegory: for these are the two covenants' (Gal 4:22,24). This a double reference in words.

A 'symbol' is a double reference in object or action, the truth being expressed by analogy. 'The seven stars in My right hand are the angels (or) messengers, by implication, a pastor (Strong) of the seven churches, and the seven lampstands are the seven churches' (Rev 1:20).

A 'type' is a resemblance between two persons or objects, represented not in words but in action. A type generally refers to something future, another double reference with two uses, one literal and one figurative. 'Now all these things happened unto them as examples (or) types (Strong), and they were written for our admonition' (1 Cor 10:11).

THE LAW OF FIRST REFERENCE

THE FIRST MENTION of a promise or figure of speech and the meaning given to it will generally establish its significance thereafter. The book of Genesis is the seed plot of the Bible where all major doctrines are first mentioned in seed form. These seeds then grow into great trees spreading their branches, their fruit and foliage all through the pages of Scripture.

The New Testament is the commentary of the Holy Spirit on the Old Testament and therefore, has the authority to restate and interpret what was said in the Old Testament. This is called the New Testament development of Old Testament themes.

When God first said to Abraham 'I will bless those who bless you and curse him who curses you' (Gen 12:3) this promise must be understood in light of the New Testament interpretation. 'To Abraham and to his Seed were the promises made. He does not say 'To seeds' as of many, but as of one, 'And to your Seed who is **Christ**' (Gal 3:16). Whether we bless or curse Abraham or Israel is not the point. **Christ** is the point!

When Abram was first told to 'Lift up your eyes and look north, south, east and west…for all the land which you see I give to you' (Gen 13:14,15) the question is, how much 'land' did Abram see? The Holy Spirit interprets this by saying 'the promise that he would be heir of the world…was through faith' (Rom 4:13). Through the eye of faith, Abraham could see the whole 'earth' - which is used all four times in that passage. He said, I'll take it all by faith! And he's still waiting for the promise…

In a Song of Ascents, 'The Lord has sworn in truth to David, He will not turn from it: I will set upon your throne the fruit of your body' (Psa 132:11). Again the Holy Spirit interprets this by saying, 'God had sworn with an oath that of the fruit of (David's) body…He would raise up Christ to sit on his throne…he spoke concerning the resurrection of Christ' (Act 2:30,31).

When some said, 'Whatever could this mean?' (Act 2:12) and Peter said, 'This is that' (Act 2:16) sometimes you would never dream 'this' is what was meant in the Old Testament! (Jol 2:28,29). The New Covenant must be allowed to override what was said in the Old, and to have the last Word. The New Testament is the final authority.

PARALLEL PASSAGES

MANY LESSONS, parables, doctrines and subjects of Scripture are recorded in parallel passages with minor differences and emphasis. A comparison of these passages leads and guides into more truth. Jesus 'spoke many things unto them in parables - that is, stories by way of proverb, symbol, figure, comparison, to throw alongside' (Mat 13:3 Amp, Strong).

Words or phrases difficult to understand in one passage, become clearer and more lucid when compared with additional statements in parallel passages. This is 'comparing spiritual things with spiritual' (1 Cor 3:13). Only by 'comparing' Scripture with Scripture can we come to the truth. There are several different kinds of parallels.

Thought parallel is where one idea is expressed in two or more different ways. Wisdom personified cries out 'I have called and you refused' (Prv 1:24). The same thought is conveyed by saying 'They refused to walk in His law' (Psa 78:10).

Word parallels help us discover the intended meaning of ambiguous or obscure words. For instance, 'Kiss the Son lest He be angry and you perish' (Psa 2:12). When this is compared with 'He who gives a right answer, kisses the lips' (Prv 24:26) the 'kiss' is interpreted as giving a 'right answer'.

David said, 'Out of the mouth of babes you have ordained **strength**' (Psa 8:2) and Jesus explains this by saying 'Out of the mouth of babes you have perfected **praise**' (Mat 21:16).

Luke says, 'If anyone comes to Me and does not **hate** his father and mother, wife and children…he cannot be my disciple' (Lk 14:26). But Matthew says, 'He who **loves** father or mother, son or daughter more than Me is not worthy of Me' (Mat 10:37). The 'hate' can then safely be interpreted to mean 'love less' than his family. This discipleship is about **love**, not **hate**!

Doctrinal parallels are found in most of Jesus' parables. Romans and Galatians both teach Justification by Faith. Paul's conversion is told three times in Acts 9, 22 and 26. There are many parallel teachings in Ephesians and Colossians. The priesthood of believers is taught in Hebrews 5 and 1 Peter 2, the body of Christ is taught in both 1 Corinthians 12 and Romans 12.

Matthew says, 'Then there shall be **great tribulation** such as has not been since the beginning of the world' (Mat 24:21). Luke restates those words by saying 'There will be **great distress** and wrath upon this people' (Lk 21:23). Matthew continues, '**When** you see the abomination of desolation…then let those who are in Judea flee to the mountains' (Mat 24:15,16).

Luke explains the same words by saying, '**When** you see Jerusalem surrounded by armies **then** know its desolation is near. Then let those who are in Judea flee to the mountains…' (Lk 21:29,21). Titus surrounded Jerusalem with his armies in 70 AD and left the gates open for three days to let any who wished to leave do so.

Josephus says all believing Jews fled to the mountains and then the gates were closed. They laid siege to the city and when it finally fell, Jerusalem was raised to the ground. Not one stone was left on top of another in the Jewish temple. The 'abomination of desolation' was complete.

Historical parallels refer to two records of the same incident or things that happened in the 'process of time'. They also refer to two prophets who prophesied a similar message to the same people at the same time.

Moses recounts the history of creation in Genesis 1 and then retells the story in Genesis 2. The Exodus is carefully chronicled, then because they didn't get it the first time it's repeated in the book of Deuteronomy. The word itself means 'repetition' (Deu 17:18). First and Second Chronicles are parallel to both books of Samuel and the Kings. Psalm 18 and 1 Samuel 22 are parallel passages.

Progressive Parallels. Parallel **visions** need to be compared in order to see the whole picture. Daniel 10:6 and Ezekiel 10 are parallels, also Ezekiel 1:5-28 and Revelation 4:2-11. Scripture will often stop, back up and start all over again, like a television 'replay' in order to retell the story.

The book of Revelation is a series of seven parallel prophetic visions of the same Gospel or Church age, sometimes referred to as the Inter-Advent Period. They're word pictures taken from different angles, highlighting different subjects. These seven visions provide a full and complete picture of what is going on in the 'last days'.

Seven times the book starts with the resurrection, runs right through to the second coming of Christ, then stops, backs up to the resurrection and starts all over again. By the time we get to chapter 20, everything has been studied except the decline and doom of the kingdom of Satan. The great climactic end of the world and total dissolution of the material universe happens at the end of each vision.

Progressive Parallelism suggests that every time we get to the second coming of Christ, the climactic emphasis increases until chapters 19 and 20 are like the mighty, explosive fortissimo of praise in Psalm 150.

God spoke to Job from the terrifying roar of a tornado saying 'the morning stars **sang** together and all the sons of God **shouted** for joy...when the sea burst forth and issued from the womb' (Job 38:7,8). After the waters broke the earth was born like a baby. If the world was created to singing and shouts of joy, it will also end with singing and a great 'shout' (1 Ths 4:18)!

The seven visions are:

1. Christ the High Priest
Revelation 1-3 (7 Churches)

2. Christ the Lamb on His Throne
Revelation 4-7 (7 Seals)

3. Christ the Judge on His Throne
Revelation 8-11 (7 Trumpets)

4. Christ the Victorious Man-Child
Revelation 12-14 (7 Mystic Figures)

5. Christ the Avenger
Revelation 15-16 (7 Bowls of Wrath)

6. Christ the Conqueror
Revelation 17-19 (7 Great Enemies)

7. Christ the King & Bridegroom
Revelation 20-22 (7 New Things)

THE HOUSE KEY

FIGURATIVE PASSAGES ARE like a house with front and back doors. They usually have a hidden key within the passage itself that will unlock and open up the message. The key to each one is close to a door, sometimes the front door, other times near the back door, under the mat, in the flower box or maybe the mailbox. The student is tasked with finding the key and using it properly.

In the 'Revelation of Jesus Christ' that key is right in the keyhole of the front door! That's the safest possible place. Who would ever look there? Jesus said, 'the thief comes to steal' (Jn 10:10) so don't let the enemy steal your key!

The key to the whole book is in the very first verse. The word 'signified' (Rev 1:1) meaning 'to communicate, indicate, intimate, mark by signs or signals, to have a deeper meaning, to represent' (Strong, Kittel, Weymouth) governs the way we read the book.

This unlocks and makes it possible to open up the whole truth. The whole of the New Testament likewise begins with 'the genealogy of Jesus Christ' (Mat 1:1) in the very first verse. That's the key to understanding everything that follows.

The key to unlocking the vision in Revelation 21 is when an angel said 'Come, I will show you the Bride, the Lamb's wife...and he showed me the great city, the holy Jerusalem' (Rev 21:9,10). We all know the 'Bride' of Christ is the church (Eph 5:32) and so the 'great city' described in the rest of Revelation 21 is the church.

The key to unlocking the mystery that swirls around Ezekiel's wheels began to be revealed when he said, 'I heard the wheels being called 'the whirling wheels'' (Ezk 10:13 NIV). Then he understood what he heard and said, 'These were the living creatures I had seen by the Chebar River, and I realized they were the cherubim' (Ezk 10:20 NIV).

INTERPRETING SYMBOLS AND FIGURES OF SPEECH

WE HAVE ALREADY SAID the Scriptures are replete with symbols and figures of speech. God used plain, 'apparent' or what is sometimes called literal language to transcribe historical and biographical records.

However it is clearly stated, the prophets, the parables of Jesus and the book of Revelation use a different form of speech (Num 12:6-8; Hos 12:10; Rev 1:1). A figure of speech or symbol is when one thing is used to represent something else. It's when a word or an object denotes something other than itself. This is called 'representative' (Rev 1:1 Kittel) speech or 'figurative language' (Jn 16:25).

How do you know when 'figurative language' is being used? Observe and apply the principle stated by God when He said, 'I have spoken to you repeatedly (NBV) by the prophets, I have multiplied visions, I have given symbols through the witness of the prophets' (Hos 12:10 NKJ). When studying the prophets, learn to expect pictures, symbols and figures of speech.

Consider the context and scope, which is the over-all intention or purpose of the writer. This will govern how you understand what is being said. Also compare parallel passages to see how they compliment one another. Allow the Scripture to determine which hermeneutic is being used and follow that principle throughout the passage, from beginning to end.

Learn to follow the passage or subject through consistently. Symbols and figures of speech generally retain the same meaning throughout Scripture. However, the 'Lion' is applied to both Christ and Satan so the same symbol is occasionally used to describe two different objects.

A symbol must symbolize, that is, the symbol must represent or denote an object other than itself. The meaning of the symbol is given to it by the Scriptures themselves. When all passages using the same symbol are carefully considered and compared, the similarity will clearly reveal the meaning of that symbol.

Sometimes it is evident from the words themselves, that symbolic language is being used. Observe words and phrases such as 'the appearance of', 'as it were', 'likeness' and 'like unto'. A similarity, resemblance or analogy is essential in the interpretation of symbols. A dragon is never a Savior (Rev 12:9). White is never evil or sin (Psa 51:7). Black is never good or righteous (Lam 4:6-8).

A clue to help in determining the extent of figurative language, is to note when the symbol or figure is dropped and the actual object takes its place. In Revelation 20, the dragon was bound with a chain, then cast into a bottomless pit and a lake. If we are going to be consistent, these must all be symbols.

However, it was not a dragon but Satan himself who was cast into 'the vengeance of eternal fire' (Jud 7). This is not literal natural or earthly fire but is nevertheless the real and true fire that never dies. Symbols as used in the Bible, must be carefully and correctly interpreted if the meaning which God intended is to be understood.

WORD PICTURES

THE REVELATION of Jesus Christ is clothed in figures of speech, symbols and metaphors. Christ is compared to and called a lion and a lamb (Rev 5:5,6), a vine (Jn 15:1) a branch (Zec 3:8), a root (Rev 22:16), a tree (SOS 2:3), a door (Jn 10:9), the way (Jn 14:6), a rock (1 Cor 10:4), a foundation (1 Cor 3:11), a star (Rev 22:16), the sun (Mal 4:2), a bridegroom (Mk 2:19) and a builder (Mat 16:18).

The church is referred to as a woman (Rev 12:1), a virgin (2 Cor 11:2), a bride (Rev 21:9), a wife (Eph 5:32), a mother (Gal 4:6), a body (1 Cor 12:27), a building (1 Cor 3:9), a house (1 Tim 3:15; Heb 3:6), a city (Mat 5:14), a temple (2 Cor 6:16) and candlesticks (Rev 1:20).

Saints or believers are like sheep (Jn 10:27), eagles (Isa 40:31), wheat (Mat 13:30), willows (Isa 44:3,4), palm trees (Psa 92:12), salt (Mat 5:13), seed (Mat 13:38), light (Mat 5:16), vessels (2 Cor 4:7); 2 Tim 2:20), soldiers (2 Tim 2:3), athletes (1 Cor 9:24); Heb 12:1), pilgrims (Heb 11:13) and priests (1 Pet 2:9).

Daniel the prophet refers to a 'stone cut out without hands' (Dan 2:34) and a 'great mountain that filled the whole earth' (Dan 2:35) which refer to Christ and His kingdom. The lion, bear, leopard, goat and ram are all used as symbols of men and nations.

Ezekiel reveals truth in the 'riddles' and 'parables' (Ezk 17:2) of a vine, sour grapes, lions' whelps, a boiling pot, dry bones, wheels full of eyes and hair bound in his skirt.

Isaiah speaks of valleys being lifted up, hills made low, trees clapping their hands and a basket of spoiled figs.

The Apostle John clothes truth in 'figurative language' using the 'signals' or 'symbols' of candlesticks, four beasts, a sealed scroll, a slain lamb, four horses, an army of locusts, a huge red dragon, many waters, Gog and Magog, a bride and a city.

Some of these 'symbols' are interpreted. The candlesticks are churches, the Lion of Judah and the Lamb of God are Jesus Christ, the locusts are demons, the dragon is Satan, the 144,000 are the redeemed of all ages, the waters are people, the horns are kings, the bride is the church, the city is the New Jerusalem and Gog and Magog are nations of the whole earth.

DUST AND DEITY

THE KEY to unlocking and interpreting the Godhead is given when Jesus said, 'These things I have spoken unto you in figurative language, but the time is coming when I will no longer speak unto you in figurative language, but I will tell you plainly about the Father' (Jn 16:25 NKJ).

Kenneth Wuest[1] says: 'These things I have spoken unto you by way of illustration in similes and comparisons. An hour is coming when no longer in similes and comparisons will I speak to you, but plainly, without the use of similes and comparisons I will tell you concerning the Father' (Jn 16:25).

The Amplified says: 'I have told you these things in parables (veiled language, allegories, dark sayings). The hour is coming when I shall no longer speak to you in figures of speech, but I shall tell you about the Father in plain words and openly - without reserve' (Jn 16:25).

This key is towards the end, that is, near the back door of extensive teaching Jesus gives concerning His relationship as the Son of God the Father (Gal 1:3). Both in the Old Testament, in the New Testament and especially in the gospel of John, Jesus indicates that He used plural, personal pronouns to describe His relationship with God.

Jesus said these plural pronouns are 'figurative language, veiled language, allegories, dark sayings similes and comparisons' (NKJ, Amp, Wuest). 'Unfortunately, the early Church lost this key so they used the literal hermeneutic and came to a very superficial and artificial conclusion at the Council of Nicaea in 325 AD.

They also developed the doctrine that Jesus Christ is the 'eternal' Son of God when the Scripture expressly states that 'God gave His only **begotten** Son' (Jn 3:16) to the world. However, if we restore and recover the key Christ gave us, this generation can use it to unlock, understand and properly interpret these 'comparisons'. They can use this key to arrive at a more accurate and realistic conclusion than the traditional, trinitarian position taken by the Church in 325 AD.

Applying the Principle

For instance, the 'figure' of water baptism is associated in the same sentence with 'Jesus Christ who is gone into heaven and is at the right hand of God, angels and authorities and powers having been made subject to Him' (1 Pet 3:21,22 KJV).

'The right hand of God' is a 'figure' of speech that indicates 'the **man** Christ Jesus' (1 Tim 2:5) is now in the place of 'power and authority'. This is confirmed when Jesus faced the Sanhedrin and said, 'the Son of Man will sit on the right hand of the power of God' (Lk 22:69). God did not choose an angel, He chose a 'Man' - one of us, to sit on the throne of the universe!

When Jesus said, 'the time is coming' He pointed to the great dispensational change about to take place. He said, 'Until now you have asked nothing in My name' (Jn

16:24) so no one had ever yet prayed **'in Jesus' Name'**. That was about to change, because 'in that day you **will** ask in My name' (Jn 16:26).

At the same time, He said He would 'tell you about the Father in plain words and openly - without reserve'. Jesus said, 'I will pray the Father and He will give you another (or) **different** (Strong) Helper (or) Standby (Amp) that He may abide with you forever - (Jn 14:16)'.

What is the **difference**? Most of what we know about Jesus has been learned from what He did during 'the days of His flesh' (Heb 5:7). 'We have known Christ after the flesh' (2 Cor 5:16) and not after the Spirit. That too, was about to change, because 'from now on...we know Him thus no longer' (2 Cor 5:16 NKJ).

The presence of Jesus was about to change from the flesh to the Spirit, from dust to Deity, and that is the difference! He said, 'A little while longer and the world will see Me no more, but **you** will see Me because...I will **manifest** Myself' (Jn 14:19,21) to you in the Spirit - not in the flesh.

TRUTH LIBERATES YOUR LIFE

❧

'YOU SHALL KNOW the truth and the truth shall make you free' (Jn 8:32). Christ came to deliver and set us free from all bondage. When the Bible is rightly understood and interpreted the truth that is taught makes men free from fear, tradition, abortive religious ritual and the powers of darkness.

Jesus said, 'You do err, not knowing the Scriptures nor the power of God' (Mat 22:29). Those Scriptures **were** the Old Testament. Paul wrote more than half the New Testament and said, 'I continue...saying **none other things** than Moses and the prophets did say would come' (Act 26:22). All truth is based on the Old Testament - then fully revealed and developed in the New.

Peter said there would be 'false teachers...who secretly bring in **fatal** heresies (Wey), even denying the Lord that bought them' (2 Pet 2:1). This is the one and only definition of 'heresy' in the Bible. Heresy is any teaching that actually 'denies the Lord that bought them' - and it's 'fatal'!

That leaves a vast scope of doctrinal difference and disagreement open to the freedom of dissent without calling one another heretics. Down through the years people have been condemned as 'heretics' and shunned, excommunicated, persecuted, tortured, abused beyond words and burned at the stake for reasons that fall far short of that 'fatal' definition.

We are warned these 'false teachers' would 'secretly, stealthily introduce (Amp)' and 'smuggle in' (Msg) 'fatal heretical doctrines' (2 Pet 2:1 Wey, Amp). These are not heathen or pagan people. They're apostates, sons of true Christians who 'deny the Lord that bought them'.

Peter said, 'many will follow' them (2 Pet 2:2) so they're popular, even famous. Some amount to personality cults. But spiritual gifts and great crowds don't prove they're in 'the way of truth' any more than was Balaam, who prophesied true words but is listed with Cain and Korah who are 'twice dead' (Jde 11,12).

Apostate 'false teachers' are called 'wells without water, clouds carried by a tempest...dogs and sows' by nature (2 Peter 2:17,22). They're not sheep! When dealing with differences, we must learn to deal with false doctrines, false cults and outright denial differently than we do with differences among brethren who are established in the faith.

The apostates Peter alluded to also 'allure...the ones who escaped from those who live in error. While they promise them liberty they themselves are servants of corruption...for he is brought into bondage' (2 Pet 2:18,19). The false doctrines they teach begin by leading into the 'bondage' of fear and rigid legalism taught and practiced by the Galatian Church.

Grace is a teacher! 'The grace of God...**teaches** us that denying ungodliness and worldly lusts, we should live sober, righteous and godly' lives (Tit 2:11,12). Any teaching that leads to loose and careless living is not 'sound doctrine' (1 Tim 1:10).

TRUTH TRANSFORMS YOUR LIFE!

THEY WHO KNOW the truth 'purify their souls' (1 Pet 1:22). 'He who says I know (God) and does not obey His commandments is a liar, and the truth is not in him' (1 Pet 2:4 Amp). Truth dispels and dissolves fear. That doesn't always happen instantly.

The process of 'line upon line, precept upon precept, here a little, there a little' (Isa 28:10) is a **progressive** revelation of truth. There is a movement in Scripture, that is ever onward and upward. This **progression** of truth is not static but at the same time, it is 'forever settled in heaven' (Psa 119:89). 'The word of our God shall stand forever' (Isa 40:8).

Truth sanctifies your life! Jesus prayed, 'Sanctify them by Your truth, your Word is truth' (Jn 17:17). The doctrines of the Bible, when correctly understood and interpreted, produce both the desire and ability to walk righteously before God and man. A right understanding of God's Word will lead to godly living and a holy life.

The sanctification produced by truth is not the 'outward appearance' (1 Sam 16:7) which stems from fear and rigid discipline, but the happy, free will outgrowth of a changed heart. 'The sanctification of the Spirit for obedience' (1 Pet 1:2) is the fruit of an inward life that is in loving submission to God.

Many today who live in error 'through fear...are all their lifetime subject to bondage' (Heb 2:15). 'Fear involves torment' (1 Jn 4:18 NKV) so we need to 'stand fast therefore, in the liberty by which Christ has made us free and be not entangled again with the yoke of bondage' (Gal 5:1).

Peter was in 'bondage' in prison and asleep when an angel 'struck him on the side' (Act 12:7). There was a sudden awakening. He obeyed the command to arise and 'his chains fell off' - so **obedience** is the liberating secret!

The chains, soldiers, guards, door, first post, second post and iron gate were all systematically and progressively removed until he was completely set free. When Peter talks about escaping 'those who live in error' (2 Pet 2:18) for a life of 'liberty' he knows what he's talking about!

PROOF OF THE TRUTH

No DOCTRINE or theological statement should ever be established from one verse or text. To discover the whole truth, we must take the sum of all Scriptures on a given subject. All divine revelation must be witnessed to by more than one writer.

God Himself laid down this principle: 'One witness shall not rise against a man...by the mouth of two or three witnesses the matter shall be established (or) **confirmed** (NAS)' (Deu 19:15). The Lord again required 'the testimony of two or three witnesses' (Deu 17:6) to prove the truth of a case. 'Anyone who kills a person is to be put to death as a murderer only on the testimony of witnesses. But no one is to be put to death on the testimony of only one witness' (Num 35:30 NIV).

Jesus said, 'If I bear witness of Myself My witness is not true. There is another who bears witness of Me...John has borne witness...but I have a greater witness than John's' (Jn 5:31-33,36). Jesus leaned on the fact that He had other witnesses to what He said and did. He said If My witness stands by itself, that is proof I don't have the truth. Christ confirmed the Law by saying 'that by the mouth of two or three witnesses every word may be established' (Mat 18:16).

Paul said to Timothy, 'Do not receive an accusation against an elder except from two or three witnesses' (1 Tim 5:19). Timothy was told not to listen to an accusation unless the accuser brings two or three witnesses to establish what he said. As soon as someone is required to make an accusation in front of other witnesses, he will say it differently.

When Paul dealt with turmoil caused by immorality in the Corinthian church he insisted, that 'by the mouth of two or three witnesses every word shall be established' (2 Cor 13:1). God holds Himself accountable by saying 'men indeed swear by the greater and an oath for confirmation is for them an end of all dispute. Thus God... confirmed the hope set before us by...two immutable things in which it is impossible for God to lie' (Heb 6:16-18).

Jesus said to the church at Ephesus 'I know your works, your labor, your patience and that you cannot bear those who are evil. You have tested those who say they are apostles and are not - and have found them liars. You have persevered, (you) have patience, (you) have labored for My name's sake and have not become weary. Nevertheless, I have this against you, that you have left your first love' (Rev 2:2-4).

The Ephesians deliberately 'left (their) first love'. They did not lose it. They made a conscious, definite decision to harden their hearts and prioritize truth at the great expense of not loving those 'evil liars'. Fervent zeal in the pursuit of truth can so easily overwhelm our love for the Lord and His people, including sinners.

Peter had to have his own heart corrected so he knew all about loving God and the sheep of His pasture. He said 'Above all, keep fervent in your love for one another, because love covers a multitude of sins' (1 Pet 4:8). We need to keep our hearts warm and soft and open towards one another in spite of it all. David cried, 'Create in me a clean heart O God and renew a right spirit within me' (Psa 51:10).

JESUS BORE WITNESS TO THE TRUTH

SCRIPTURE REFERS TO 'JESUS CHRIST, the faithful witness' (Rev 1:5) and further reveals Him as 'the Amen, the Faithful and True witness' (Rev 19:11). John earlier stated that 'truth came by Jesus Christ' (Jn 1:17). Paul said in Him 'are hidden all the treasures of wisdom and knowledge' (Col 2:3).

When 'Pilate said to Him 'What is truth?'' (Jn 18:38) he asked the wrong question. It's very hard to give a right answer if people insist on asking the wrong question. But Jesus said 'For this cause I was born, and for this cause I came into the world, that I should bear witness to the truth' (Jn 18:37). Truth is not a 'what' or a thing. Truth is a Person! The whole body of revealed truth stood right in front of Pilate and he couldn't see it for looking.

Jesus said, 'I **am** the truth' (Jn 14:6). What a tremendous statement is this! Here is the gold standard of truth, a positive test by which our doctrine can be examined. Did Jesus bear witness to that which we teach and believe to be the truth? The gospel records reveal that Jesus confirmed by His own teaching, every major doctrine taught in the Old and New Testaments.

Jesus verified salvation by faith, the necessity of atoning blood, water baptism, baptism in the Holy Spirit, the church, the Kingdom of God, His second advent, physical resurrection of the just and unjust, heaven and hell. He referred to the Old Testament as 'truth' (Jn 17::17) and spoke of the 'Law of Moses, the Prophets and the Psalms' (Lk 24:44).

The words of Jesus are replete with quotations from, and allusions to, the Old Testament. Many of the passages attacked by unbelievers are treated by Christ as being authentic. The Genesis account of creation (Mat 19:4), the flood (Lk 17:27), the destruction of Sodom (Lk 17:29), death of Lot's wife (Lk 17:32), Jonah and the 'great fish' (Mat 12:40) and the cleansing of Naaman (Lk 4:27) are all verified.

Christ also spoke of Abel (Lk 11:51), Abraham, Isaac and Jacob (Mat 22:31), Moses and the burning bush (Lk 20:37), manna in the wilderness (Jn 6:30,32,49), the brazen serpent (Jn 3:14), Elijah and Elisha (Lk 4:25).

The silence of Jesus on any subject exposes that subject to be lacking in truth. We should therefore seriously question any doctrine or subject that we accept as truth, if we cannot confirm it in the testimony of Him who came to bear witness to the truth.

Jesus as the 'Faithful and True witness' not only confirmed truth but also exposed error by saying 'You do err, not knowing the Scriptures nor the power of God' (Mat 22:29). He warned the multitudes including His disciples and lashed out at the 'scribes and Pharisees' for their hypocrisy and deception - then concluded by saying, 'You are witnesses against yourselves' (Mat 23:1-31; Mk 7:6-23).

TRUTH IS CHRIST CENTERED

JESUS CHRIST IS the hidden treasure and main theme of all Scripture. He is the truth of God embodied in a Person. A student should always 'suspect the text' of referring to Jesus unless statements or details clearly indicate otherwise.

The Scripture is the written Word, the Word in a book. 'I, the Lord, have written excellent things to you...to make you know the certainty of the Words of truth' (Prv 22:19-21). Jesus is the living Word of God - the Word in flesh. 'The Word became flesh, dwelt among us' (Jn 1:14) and walked all over the hills of Galilee.

The Scriptures testify of Christ. 'Beginning at Moses and all the Prophets, He **expounded** to them in all the

Scriptures the things concerning Himself...that all things must be fulfilled which were written in the Law of Moses and the Prophets and the Psalms concerning Me' (Lk 24:27,44).

'Philip said, 'We have found Him of whom Moses and the law, and also the prophets wrote - Jesus of Nazareth" (Jn 1:45). 'To Him all the prophets witness that...whoever believes in Him will receive remission of sins' (Act 10:44). 'Then I said, Behold, I have come - in the volume (the whole) of the book it is written of Me - to do Your will, O God' (Heb 10:7).

The books of Moses or the Pentateuch, the Psalms, **all** the Prophets, the Gospels, Acts, the Epistles and Revelation are all a great unfolding and unveiling of Christ. He is the central theme or thesis and main subject of all Scripture. All other subjects are used only in their relationship to Jesus Christ.

'Worship God! For the testimony of Jesus is the spirit of prophecy' (Rev 19:10). 'Those things which God foretold by the mouth of all His prophets...that He may send Jesus Christ...which **God has spoken** by the mouth of all His holy prophets since the world began' (Act 3:18,20,21).

'Apollos, an eloquent man, mighty in the Scriptures... vigorously refuted the Jews, showing from the Scriptures that Jesus is the Christ' (Act 18:24,28). 'To Jesus Christ who is...by the prophetic Scriptures made known to all nations...to God alone, be glory forever. Amen.' (Rom 16:25-27).

Christ is the great High Priest of whom all other priests were but types (Heb 3:1,2), and the great Prophet of whom all others were but forerunners (Lk 7:16). He is Jacob's ladder between Heaven and earth, the door of Heaven (Jn 1:51; Gen 28:12), the Lion of Judah and Shiloh (Gen 49:9,10).

Jesus is the water-sweetening Branch (Ex 15:24,25), the bright and morning Star (2 Pet 1:19), rightful heir of the vineyard (Mat 21:37,38), tried cornerstone and sure foundation (Isa 28:16). Christ is God's covenant with men (Isa 49:8), the Sabbath rest of God (Col 2:16,17), the believer's land of promise and inheritance (Heb 3:11,14; 12:22,24). Jesus is King of kings and Lord of lords! (1 Tim 6:15).

UNDERSTANDING THE WORD OF TRUTH

THE PROBLEM we have today with finding some solution in a truth God reveals, is that we tend to focus and fixate on 'the answer'. Whole denominations are raised up that camp around a certain revelation and 'they progress no further' (2 Tim 3:9 NKJ).

One day Jesus said, Let's go fishing (Lk 5:4). Searching for truth is like fishing all over the place and finally catching a couple in a little old, unlikely looking pond. Then we say This is it! And we don't bother fishing any of the other lakes and streams because this is the only one where we ever caught anything. God wants to teach us there are some fish in all the lakes, some answers in all the truths being emphasized and revealed today.

Scripture cannot be comprehended or correctly interpreted until it relates to and reveals Jesus Christ. He is the truth, the fulfillment of the types, the main subject of the Psalms and the 'spirit' or 'vital principle' (Rev 19:10 Strong) and theme of the prophets.

Jesus is the long-promised Deliverer-Saviour, God's total provision for man's need. He is bread from Heaven (Jn 6:31-35), water flowing from the smitten rock (1 Cor 10:4), the fountain opened (Zec 13:10), the smitten Shepherd (Zec 13:7) and the risen Sun of righteousness (Mal 4:2).

'Then He said to them, 'O foolish ones and slow of heart to believe in all the prophets have spoken! ...And they said to one another, Did not our heart burn within us... while He opened the Scriptures to us? ...And He opened their understanding, that they might **comprehend** the Scriptures' (Lk 24:25,32,45).

Jesus is the seed promised to Eve, Abraham, Isaac, Jacob and David. 'Now to Abraham and his Seed were the promises made. He does not say, 'And to seeds' as of many, but as of one, 'And to your Seed who is Christ' (Gal 3:16). All genealogies ended with Him.

The book of the genealogy of Jesus Christ' lists the generations from Abraham to 'Joseph the husband of Mary, of whom was born Jesus who is called Christ' (Mat 1:1,16). Leviticus describes in detail, the five offerings by which we **get right** with God and then **come** to God. The feasts are designed for us to **keep right** with God.

The Burnt, Meal, Peace, Sin and Trespass offerings all foreshadow the coming Christ. Jesus is the Lamb of God pictured by a myriad of Old Testament offerings that all point towards and come to their complete end in Christ. 'Now where there is remission of (sins), there is no longer an offering for sin' (Heb 10:18).

The Holy Spirit came to 'teach you all things' (Jn 14:26) and 'guide you into all truth' (Jn 16:13). Jesus said when the 'Spirit of truth' comes 'He will testify of Me' (Jn 15:26) and 'will glorify Me' (Jn 16:14) by speaking and declaring the things of Christ to you. This is to 'comprehend the Scriptures'.

THY KINGDOM COME

THE GOVERNMENT of God is the same as the Kingdom of God, only not so exciting. It seems to be more along practical lines and exists anywhere God's will is known and done. The government of God is God's Word in God's man and God's people doing God's will. The Kingdom of God is central to the Christian message. It is beyond strange that none of the major creeds of the Church present the Kingdom of God as a main theme of the Gospel.

There are Covenant principles that when known and understood, make us different from the world. At Mount Sinai the Lord said, 'If you **obey Me fully** (NIV) and keep My covenant, then you shall be a special treasure to Me from among and above all people (Amp)... and you shall be to Me a kingdom of priests' (Ex 19:5,6).

The conditional promise that we would be different, that is, a 'special treasure,' depends on our full obedience.

Then Jesus came and stood in our midst with clear vision, understanding God's Covenant and its disciplines. 'He went up on a mountain and when He was seated...He opened His mouth and taught them' (Mat 5:1,2). Speaking as a prophet, He began to interpret the situation.

Matthew five, six and seven are the Constitution and Bylaws of the Kingdom of God. They are the principles that govern how we are to conduct ourselves. It's the same God, same message, same Covenant - same government and Kingdom of God, same everything but with some important **new** ingredients. All that's different is the time the place and the people.

Jesus stepped into a Jewish traditional situation that was so legal, rigid and hard He was truly a 'root out of dry ground' (Isa 53:2) - nothing but death all round. Everything was flat under the iron heel and nailed boot of Roman rule. Caesar was god.

Then John said, Hi! And Jesus said, the government of God is here. It sure didn't look like it and still doesn't. They said How can that be? Jesus said, It's John and Me. And they said, John is in prison and losing his head. But Jesus said **I'm** here…

The coming of Christ including His death and resurrection, marks the end of the **Old** Covenant in which God 'made the **first** obsolete' (Heb 8:13). Then 'He takes away the **first** that He may establish the **second**' (Heb 10:9) which is 'the **New** Covenant in My blood' (Lk 22:20) with very important **new** ingredients.

This inter-testament period of preparation and great pivotal progression of truth lifts everything from the earthly realm up into the heavenly realm (1 Cor 15:48). It divides between 'the former days' (Zec 8:11) and 'the last days' (Heb 1:2; Act 2:17). God's old economy, management and administration was replaced with a brand new 'dispensation of the grace of God' (Eph 3:2).

'Copies of the true' (Heb 9:24) that were 'symbolic for the present time' (Heb 9:9 NKJ) now moved from 'that which is natural' to 'that which is spiritual' (1 Cor 15:46), from the old 'creation' (Heb 9:11) to the new creation. 'Old things have passed away. Behold, the **fresh** and **new** has come!' (1 Cor 5:17 Amp).

'A feast day, a new moon or a sabbath...are only a shadow of things to come, and they have only a symbolic value. But the reality - the substance, the solid fact of what is foreshadowed, the body of it - belongs to Christ' (Col 2:15,16 Amp). Who needs fleeting 'shadows' when we have the 'solid substance'? Or a candle when the 'Sun' shines in His strength?

Who wants abortive religious ritual where spiritually dead ministers mutter vague nothings in their musty sanctums, when we have spontaneous prophetic utterance and 'living words'? Why do we need or want Old Testament pageantry when we have New Testament power? Nowhere in the New Testament, are we allowed to pine for Old Testament provisions.

THE BATTLE AND THE BOTTLE

WHEN JESUS INSTITUTED THE 'NEW COVENANT' at the last supper with His disciples, He said 'I will not drink of the fruit of this vine **from now on until that day** when I drink it new and of superior quality (Amp) in my Father's Kingdom' (Mat 26:29).

This declaration is profoundly dispensational. That night He went to the Cross where the Old Wine was cut off and the New Wine of the Holy Spirit was poured out on 'that day' of Pentecost. On 'that day' Jesus drank deeply and has been drinking the New Wine ever since.

'The Cross of Christ' (Php 3:13) brought in an undeniable transition and change from the Old to the New, from the 'natural' to the 'spiritual'. Christians often agree that we should be drinking the New Wine but there are many 'sipping saints' who keep on with the Old, when the 'circumcision of Christ' is intended to cut it right off.

They argue that Jesus turned the water into wine (Jn 2:9) as if that was intended to govern and be the pattern for what we do today - but it's an Old Covenant provision. Some say it's not reasonable that God would add alcohol to a supernatural drink.

Paul said this was 'a **shadow** of things that were to come. The **substance** is found **in Christ**' (Col 2:17 NKJ). Even in the Old Testament we are repeatedly warned that 'wine is a mocker, strong drink is raging, and whoever is deceived thereby is not wise' (Prv 20:21).

Solomon gives a classic and detailed description of alcoholism. He concludes by saying, 'At the last it bites like a serpent and stings like an adder...You will say They struck me, but I was not hurt! They beat me but I did not feel it! When shall I awake that I may seek another drink?' (Prv 23:29-35 Amp).

Medical people are saying openly these days, that even a small amount of alcohol contributes to several kinds of cancer. The Bible says, 'An overseer **must** give no grounds for accusation, **must** be above reproach and **not given** to wine' (1 Tim 3:2,3 Amp). Strong says 'not given' means to be 'not near or in the vicinity of, above and beyond, contrary to, opposed to, **against**'.

Anyone in Christian leadership '**must** be...opposed to' and '**against**' drinking alcohol in any amount. 'The Cross of Christ' (Php 3:13) **must** be applied to every area of our lives and allowed to cut off all Old Testament provisions. The endless destruction of lives, families and the carnage on highways is overwhelming practical evidence of the fruit of those doings - and should be the end of this dispute.

The prophet said, 'War-horses (NIV) and the battle bow shall be cut off, He shall speak peace to the nations, and from **the river** (Jordan) to the ends of the earth' (Zec 9:10 NIV). Jesus was baptized in Jordan and His Kingdom of peace continues spreading from there 'to the ends of the earth'.

'The battle bow' was 'cut off' at the Cross by the 'circumcision of Christ' (Col 2:11). This lifted the whole concept of warfare from the 'natural' to the 'spiritual' (1 Cor 15:46) - from the 'flesh' to the 'spirit' (Jn 3:6). 'We do not war according to the flesh' (1 Cor 10:3,4) in this dispensation.

Everyone I know seems to understand this these days. Nobody thinks the Gospel of the Kingdom should be enforced by the edge of the sword. But this has not always been the case. It was a dark day indeed when this revelation was lost about a thousand years ago. Military Crusades were launched to recapture Jerusalem by force, with disastrous consequences.

The Christian testimony has never recovered from this in some parts of the world. Warfare is obviously 'spiritual' and not 'natural' in this dispensation. The New Wine must also now be 'spiritual' and not 'natural'.

CAPITAL CRIMES

GOD SAID TO NOAH, 'Surely for your lifeblood...I will require the life of man. Whoever sheds man's blood, by man his blood shall be shed' (Gen 9:5,6). Later the Lord said to Israel, 'He who strikes a man so he dies shall surely be put to death' (Ex 21:12). This is followed with, 'You shall give life for life, eye for eye, tooth for tooth, foot for foot...' (Ex 21:23-25). These are undeniable statements of the right of victims and duty of society at that time. Some say if we lived according to these laws today, everybody would be blind, toothless and footless.

There were many notable exceptions under the Old Covenant. Cain killed Abel but 'the Lord set a mark on Cain lest anyone should kill him' (Gen 4:8,15). Levi and Simeon murdered Shechem and the men of his city (Gen 34:25,26) but they were not executed. Moses killed an

Egyptian but lived for 120 years (Ex 2:12; 34:7). Uriah the Hittite was a loyal convert to the truth, but David had him killed. The Lord was 'displeased' (2 Sam 11:27) but David lived on and died of old age (1 Kgs 1:1; 2:1). Abner killed Asahel (2 Sam 2:23), Joab and Abishai killed Abner (2 Sam 3:30), Rechab and Baanah killed Ishbosheth (2 Sam 4:6) and Absalom killed Ammon (2 Sam 13:28) but none of these were ever brought to trial in accordance with the Law of Moses.

Rabbinical interpretation of the Law required two eyewitnesses to achieve a conviction. Witnesses had to have forewarned the accused he was about to commit a capital crime. Witnesses had to be interrogated separately, and any material discrepancy led to acquittal. No circumstantial evidence and no testimony based on inference or hearsay, was admissible. The accused was presumed innocent until proven guilty, and could not be tried more than once for the same offence. If any new evidence was found, a stay of execution was automatic. 'As I live, says the Lord, I have no pleasure in the death of the wicked, but that the wicked turn from his way and live. Turn, turn from your evil ways!' (Ezk 33:11).

Murderers can 'turn and live'. Moses lived on to serve the Lord, not commit more murders. Cain never did believe in God's plan of redemption but even he, did not continue to commit more murders. The Scriptures demonstrate that murderers can be rehabilitated, and redeemed if they are willing.

When Ephesus erupted into an 'uproar' the 'city clerk' tried to teach caution when he said 'you ought to be quiet and do nothing rashly'. The 'clerk' was able to calm down the crowd and 'dismiss the assembly' (Act 19:35-36,39-40). However, there were many cases of unjust lynchings and stoning: Abiram (1 Kgs12:18), Naboth (1 Kgs 21:13), Zechariah (2 Chr 24:10,21), Stephen (Act 7:58,59), Paul (Act 14:19) and a servant (Mat 21:35).

CHANGING THE LAW

⚜

THE LAW of Moses was 'added because of transgressions, **till the Seed should come** to whom the promise was made' (Gal 3:19). When that 'Seed, which is Christ' came (Gal 3:16), the Law changed. The scribes and Pharisees brought a woman caught in the very act of adultery to Christ. They said 'Moses in the law commanded us that such should be stoned. But what do you say?' (Jn 3:3-5).

Then 'Jesus stooped down and wrote on the ground with His finger' (Jn 3:6) but what did He 'write with His finger'? He rewrote the Law just like He did as the Great 'I Am' when 'He gave Moses two tables of Testimony, tables of stone, written with the finger of God' (Ex 31:18). God's finger of flesh now 'wrote on the ground' in the same way His fiery finger of the Spirit burned the Law into stone on Mount Sinai.

'Again, He stooped down and wrote on the ground' (Jn 8:8) and what did He write this time? Now He became more focused and specific. He zeroed right in on each and every one of her accusers by writing out their own personal names in fulfilment of a prophecy.

The Word was that '**they** shall be written on the ground, because **they** have forsaken the Lord, the fountain of living waters' (Jer 17:13). 'The fountain of living waters' refers to Solomon's exhortation to 'drink water from your own cistern and running water from your own well. Why should your fountains be dispersed abroad, streams of water in the streets? Let them be only your own and not for strangers with you. Let your fountain be blessed, and rejoice with the wife of your youth' (Prv 5:15-18).

The Bible says, 'mercy and truth are met together, righteousness and peace have kissed each other' (Psa 85:10). When the Scribes and Pharisees said, 'But what do you say?' they thought they had Him cold. If He showed 'mercy' they'd say, Where's the 'truth' of the Law? If He condemned her, they'd say Where is 'mercy'?

After writing out each of their names in full before their very eyes, the 'truth' struck home and knocked them over one by one. Suddenly it was turned on them. This 'two-edged sword' became 'truth' for them, and 'mercy' for her. They could not understand that God is both, and knows how to apply them both. 'Jesus said Woman, has no one condemned you? She said, No one Lord. Jesus said to her Neither do I condemn you: go and sin no more' (Jn 8:10,11).

Jesus didn't condemn her accusers either, for all their sins. Their 'conscience' was 'convicted' (Jn 8:9) by the Holy Spirit - not condemned. This is God's last Word and final verdict on capital punishment, for all time. Jesus **is** the Lawgiver, and He can change it any time He pleases.

RIGHTLY DIVIDING THE WORD
OF TRUTH

YOUNG TIMOTHY WAS EXHORTED to be a 'workman with no cause to be ashamed, correctly interpreting the message of truth' (NBV) or 'correctly analyzing, rightly dividing - accurately handling, skilfully teaching and cutting straight the Word of Truth' (2 Tim 2:15 Amp, Strong, Thayer).

Some teachers, in their effort to 'rightly divide' the Scriptures, have chopped human history into multiple sections, covenants and dispensations, affirming that each division is distinct from the other and God has dealt differently with men in each dispensation. This so-called 'dispensationalism' is rejected by many.

God has, from the beginning of time, dealt with man on the same single principle or 'law of faith' (Rom 3:27). 'Without faith it is impossible to please Him' (Heb 11:6). 'I am the Lord I do not change' (Mal 3:6). Truth never changes. It only unfolds and continues to open up in ongoing progressive revelation throughout the Scriptures.

Scripture moves from the less to the better, from the old to the new, from types and shadows to the true substance. There is but one clearly stated division in Scripture. John the Baptist towers up as the great monument of demarcation and he it is, that introduces the inter-testament period of preparation. John understood the 'times and seasons' (1 Ths 5:1).

Jesus came and said, 'The time has come' (Mk 1:14,15 NIV). Then He said, 'What did you go out to see? A prophet? Yes, I tell you and **much more** than a prophet...there is no one greater than John' (Lk 7:26,28). 'The law and the prophets were proclaimed until John. **Since that time** the Gospel of the Kingdom is being preached' (Lk 16:16 NIV).

When a prophet says something new like speaking in tongues, deep water baptism in Jesus' Name or deliverance from demons, people make their choices. A lot of chaff is lost so the effect of the prophet is to 'sift as wheat' (Lk 22:31) and keep God's kingdom people clean and free from mixture.

John stood between the Old and New Covenants, economy, management and administration of the government or Kingdom of God. He stood at the biblical 'Great Divide' of all human history which is what makes him so '**much more** than a prophet' (Lk 16:16).

John's whole life and ministry was pointing the way and preparing people - pronouncing God's New Order. The world has never been the same, so the effect of the prophet is to make a difference. What a world changing difference John's ministry made!

THE LAW OF DOUBLE REFERENCE

SOME SCHOLARS OBJECT to this principle because they consider 'double reference' to be the same as 'double meaning'. Scripture cannot have a double meaning. Nevertheless, there is a principle of double reference or use, which must be distinguished. The confusion comes from a misunderstanding of the way types and shadows, symbols and allegories are used.

'That which is natural' and 'that which is spiritual' are presented in a definite order: 'the order is 'natural' first and then 'spiritual'' (1 Cor 15:46 JBP). This order must be diligently observed. The sequence **cannot** be reversed. Many **first** references to subjects in Scripture are presented as types or figurative object lessons in the visible, material realm.

They are called a 'copy and shadow' (Heb 8:5) of the true and real substance. These object lessons picture the **second** or 'that which is spiritual'. 'The cross of Christ' (Php 3:13) is how 'He takes away the **first** that He may **establish** the **second**' (Heb 10:9). The law of double reference often refers to two different, although related subjects, which are both called by the same name.

A Bible student must discover which one of the two, a prophet or passage is referring to. If this has not been correctly determined, a statement will be misinterpreted, or a promise misunderstood if it is applied to the natural when it belongs to the spiritual.

There are two cities - one visibly natural and earthly. The other is an invisible, spiritual and 'heavenly Jerusalem' (Heb 12:22). There are two Mount Zions, a material 'mountain that can be touched' (Heb 12:18, 22 Amp) and the other 'heavenly' mountain. There are two tabernacles (Heb 8:2; 9:8,9), two temples (1 Chr 6:10; 1 Pet 2:5), two promised lands (Heb 4:8) and two nations (Ex 19:6; 1 Pet 2:9).

We are told 'the city of our God...(is) beautiful for situation, the joy of the whole earth is Mount Zion...

walk about Zion and go all around her, count her towers, mark well her bulwarks, consider her palaces' (Psa 48:1,2).

The Holy Spirit then interprets Mount Zion by saying 'you have come to Mount Zion, city of God...to the **general assembly** and **church** of the firstborn' (Heb 12:22,23) so when you come to church, you have come to Mount Zion!

'If Joshua had given them **rest**...he would not have spoken of **another** day' (Heb 4:8). Joshua led Israel into the promised land but he said there was 'another' kind of land they needed to enter which is Christ, who said 'Come unto **Me** and I'll give you **rest**' (Mat 11:28).

When 'you come to Mount Zion...to **Jesus**' (Heb 12:22,24) you have also come to the real land of promise and rest. Mount Zion is in the land and Jesus stands on that mountain, calling us to enter in and 'partake of Christ' (Heb 3:14). Do you see the double reference here? There are two mountains and two lands. There are also two nations.

The Lord said, 'You shall be to Me a kingdom of priests, a **holy nation**' (Ex 19:6). The Holy Spirit restates this in the New Testament and interprets it by saying to the church, '**You** are a royal priesthood, a **holy nation**, His own special people...who once were not a people but are now the people of God' (1 Pet 2:9,10).

WHAT IS 'THE CIRCUMCISION'?

MOST PEOPLE UNDERSTAND physical circumcision but not everyone has even a vague understanding of the real and true 'circumcision' taught in the Scriptures. In the beginning, 'circumcision' was the sign and seal of being in covenant with God.

'This is my **covenant** which you shall keep. Every man child among you shall be circumcised' (Gen 17:10). Later Jeremiah said, 'Circumcise yourselves to the Lord, and take away the foreskins of your hearts' (Jer 4:4). Then Paul said, 'Your circumcision has become uncircumcision' (Rom 2:25) because it was not the real, true circumcision of the heart.

Finally, '**In Him** you were also circumcised with the circumcision made without hands…by the circumcision of Christ' (Col 2:11). 'The circumcision of Christ' took place at the Cross of Christ when He was cut off (Col 2:12,13). Daniel prophesied that 'Messiah shall be cut off' (Dan 9:26) and Isaiah confirmed it by saying 'He was cut off from the land of the living for the transgressions of My people' (Isa 53:8).

WHAT IS 'THE CONCISION'?

'BEWARE OF DOGS, beware of evil workers, beware of the concision' (Php 3:2 KJV) - 'Be on your guard against these curs' (JBP) - 'Look out for those dogs (the Judaizers), look out for those mischief-workers' (Amp) - 'Beware of these dogs, these wicked workmen, the incision-party!' (Moffat) - 'Beware of the mutilation!' (NKV).

These 'dogs' were not literal canines. They were metaphors for men who were bringing Christians back into bondage through teaching that is not 'safe'. Paul said, What I am going to say to you 'is not tedious, but for you it is **safe**' (Php 3:1). He said 'Better safe than sorry' so 'stay clear of barking dogs' (Php 3:1,2 Msg). These 'dogs' have teeth, they bite and cut but don't cut far enough and that is 'mutilation'.

Paul uses rough language to describe those who do not 'worship the Father in spirit, in truth' (Jn 4:23). He said, 'We are the circumcision who worship God in the spirit...and have no confidence in the flesh' (Php 3:3). We don't bite and tear at fleshly things. We cut them right off because that is the only 'safe' thing to do.

The 'evil work' of these 'Judaizers' who like 'dogs' were trying to grab and drag Christians back into Judaism and under the Law, was not in the context of immorality. Any heathen can live in moral rectitude if he chooses to do so. Paul did as a Jew, get rid of moral weakness. He did not practice living in the gutter. 'Concerning righteousness which is in the law' he was 'blameless' (Php 3:6).

These people were not enemies of Christ. They loved Christ and all His signs, wonders and miracles. They were 'enemies of the **Cross** of Christ' (Php 3:18) who like Peter 'took Him aside and began to rebuke Him, saying Far be it from You, Lord, this shall not happen to You!' (Mat 16:22).

'Peter's reaction was Satanic, that is, adversarial. This does not suggest Satan had entered Peter. Jesus said, '**You** are an offence to Me, for **you** are not mindful of the things of God, but the things of men' (Mat 16:23). 'The things of men' are the teeth in these 'dogs' that are too blunt and jagged to really cut it off.

'Concision' comes from roots meaning 'to cut, chop' or 'hack' (Strong). Instead of 'rightly dividing' or 'cutting straight the word of truth' (2 Tim 2:15 Strong, Thayer) this chopping, hacking action tears away at the Scriptures and 'mutilates' the message.

The only alternative is to 'rightly divide' the Scriptures. It indicates a straight line 'rising perpendicularly, upright and erect' intersected by another 'level, horizontal' (Strong, Thayer) line forming the sign of the 'Cross'. The Cross with its scissor like action became a sharp instrument, a cross cutting knife in the hand of God to perform 'the circumcision of Christ' (Col 2:11).

This great 'circumcision' not only 'cut off Messiah' (Dan 9:26) but the old covenant economy and management, replacing it with this brand new 'dispensation of the grace of God' (Eph 3:2) in which we now live. 'Old things have passed away. **Behold** - the **fresh** and **new** has come!' (2 Cor 5:17 Amp).

The Cross of Christ lifts everything from the earthly realm up into the heavenly realm (1 Cor 15:48). 'Copies of the true' (Heb 9:24) that were 'symbolic for the present time' (Heb 9:9 NKJ) now moved from 'that which is natural' to 'that which is spiritual' (1 Cor 15:46), from the old 'creation' (Heb 9:11) to the new creation.

EARTHLY - HEAVENLY - REALMS

EARTHLY + HEAVENLY

Old (Heb 8:13) + New (Heb 8:13)

Natural (1 Cor 15:46) + Spiritual (1 Cor 15:46)

Copies (Heb 9:24 NKV) + True (Heb 9:24 NKJ)

Earthly (1 Cor 15:49 KJV) + Heavenly (1 Cor 15:49 KJV)

Flesh (Jn 3:6) + Spirit (Jn 3:6)

Seen (2 Cor 4:18) + Unseen (2 Cor 4:18)

Visible (2 Cor 4:18) + Invisible (2 Cor 4:18)

Temporal (Cor 4:18) + Eternal (2 Cor 4:18)

First (Heb 8:7) + Second (Heb 10:9)

Taken Away (Heb 10:9) + Established (Heb 10:9)

Shadow (Col 2:16,17 NKJ) + Substance (Col 2:16,17 NKJ)

Resemblance (Heb 10:1 Strong) + Reality (Heb 10:1 Strong)

Made With Hands (Heb 9:24) + Made Without Hands (Heb 9:11)

Testimony (Heb 3:5) + Good Things (Heb 10:1)

Letter (2 Cor 3:6) + Spirit (2 Cor 3:6)

Written With Ink (2 Cor 3:3) + Written by the Spirit (2 Cor 3:3)

Tables of Stone (2 Cor 3:6) + Tables of Flesh/Heart (2 Cor 3:3)

Born of the Flesh (Jn 3:6) + Born of the Spirit (Jn 3:6)

Natural Children (Rom 9:8) + God's Children (Rom 9:8 NIV)

Not Israel (Rom 9:6,8) + Israel of God (Gal 6:16)

Jewish Nation (Act 10:22) + Holy Nation (1 Pet 2:9)

Foreign Country (Heb 11:9 NKJ) + Heavenly Country (Heb 11:16 KJV)

Promised Land (Heb 11:9) + Another Land (Heb 4:8)

Mount Sinai (Gal 4:24,25) + Mount Zion (Heb 12:18,22)

No Continuing City (Heb 13:14) + Eternal City (Isa 60:14,15)

First Tabernacle (Heb 9:8) + True Tabernacle (Heb 8:2))

Temple Buildings (Mat 24:1) + Temple of God (1 Cor 3:16)

Levitical Priesthood (Heb 7:11) + Royal Priesthood (1 Pet 2:9)

Vain Worship (Mk 7:7) + True Worship (Jn 4:23)

Dead Sacrifices (Heb 9:9) + Living Sacrifices (Rom 12:1)

Fleshly Washing (Heb 9:9) + Washing of Regeneration (Tit 3:5)

Old Wine (Lk 5:39) + New Wine (Mat 26:29)

Physical War (2 Cor 10:4) + Spiritual War (2 Cor 19:4)

Human Weapons (2 Cor 10:3 Amp) + Armor of God (Eph 6:11)

Worldly Kingdoms (Jn 18:36) + Kingdom of God (Lk 17:20,21)

Throne of Israel (1Kgs 9:5) + Throne of God (Heb 12:2)

THE CROSS POINT

'THE CROSS OF CHRIST' (Php 3:13) performed the great 'circumcision of Christ' (Col 2:11) which completely cut off the Old and brought in the New. The Cross is the equilibrium of the universe! The Cross cut off and canceled all the old influences resulting in an unchanging, balanced and stable system going forward. The Cross is the most powerful principle in the universe!

No other belief system on the face of the earth has, or ever **has** had, anything like the Judeo-Christian revelation of 'the Cross of Christ'. The principles of the Cross change everything, including the way we see ourselves, the world and God Himself. You cannot see God through 'moral' eyes, only through the 'blood of His cross' (Col 1:20).

'The blood of His cross' (Col 1:20) is not for you, but for God. Armageddon is a picnic compared to what happened at the Cross. Stay at the Cross! Because that's where the Judgment fell, and that fire can never fall there again. It's the only 'safe' place (Php 3:1). It's the one and only sacrifice that makes what we offer, acceptable to God.

The Bible says, 'make no provision for the flesh' (Rom 13:14). When you complain to the pastor about some sore in your flesh, his first duty should be to tell you to drop dead! The only provision God makes for the flesh is the Cross.

Samson's power was not 'safe' in his hands because there was no cross point in his life. Do we suppose living 'in the flesh' is good? If the Devil went away on vacation our flesh would make such a mess of things, we'd all land in jail before the week was up.

We are not saved by His sacrificial death. We are 'saved by His life' (Rom 5:10). We need someone who is **alive** - who can pull us up out of the deep miry clay, the ditch - the mud and filth of the sewer into which all mankind has fallen.

The entire fabric of 'righteousness' was woven on the loom of the Cross (Php 3:9). All the ages of eternity revolve around the Cross. The Cross is the centre and circumference of all God's purposes. What God did in the past was because the Cross was coming. What God will do in the future is because the Cross came.

These are days of transition and change. Anyone who successfully passes through them will have to embrace the Cross, not dance around it. If we decide to go through with living a crucified life, the pressure comes on, the warfare intensifies, and the Cross appears.

Kiss the Cross! And come away with a mouth full of splinters. It will change the way you speak and live. When Jesus wrestled with 'this cup' (Mat 26:39) in the garden, God's whole economy shifted and changed. He said, 'Fear not, it is your Father's good pleasure to give you the kingdom' (Lk 11:32). If we really embrace the Cross, we'll see it come.

CHEMISTRY OF THE BLOOD

$$\text{\emph{caligraphic ornament}}$$

'THE WORD OF GOD IS ALIVE' (Heb 4:12). The average life of the average book is 10 years, but the Bible never dies and will never become obsolete. Why? Because the message of the 'blood' circulates through its pages. Take that out and it dies like every other book.

'The life (nephesh) of the flesh is in the blood' (Lev 17:11). 'Its blood sustains it' (Lev 17:14). 'The Lord breathed into (Adam) the breath of life and man became a living soul (nephesh)' (Gen 2:7). So 'blood' is closely associated with 'breath'. When God breathed into Adam He started the process of absorbing oxygen into blood, without which no man can live.

Five quarts of blood circulate every 23 seconds. Five million red cells per cubic milligram carry life giving food and oxygen to every cell, then carry garbage away in the same vehicle with no contamination. Blood is our only mobile tissue. It connects and inter-relates every member of the body, making them 'members one of another' (Eph 4:25).

Christ made us blood relatives by His 'blood of the new covenant' (Mat 26:28) but we often act like we're just related by ordinary human blood. 'You were not redeemed with corruptible things but with the precious blood of Christ' (1 Pet 1:18,19).

'He foreseeing this, that His soul was not left in Hades, nor did His flesh see corruption' (Act 2:31). Why not? Because the 'blood of Christ' is 'incorruptible'. Had Jesus not laid down His life, He would still be alive today. Corruptible blood makes pimples, boils and allows decomposition, like Lazarus whose dead body produced a 'stench' (Jn 11:39 NAS).

Judas said, 'I have betrayed innocent blood' (Mat 27:4). The angel said 'that holy thing...shall be called the Son of God' (Lk 1:35) so His blood is both 'innocent, holy' and 'incorruptible'. God said, 'In the day you eat of the tree...you shall surely die' (Gen 2:7). When man ate it, he injected a potent poison into his bloodstream that made human blood sinful, and death became inevitable. How could all this be?

'As children are partakers (koinoneo) of flesh and blood, He also Himself likewise took part (metecho) of the same' (Heb 2:14). 'Koinoneo' means 'to partner, share with flesh AND blood' (Thayer). 'Metecho' Vine says, 'is less thorough in effect than the former'.

The Bible is saying Jesus' blood was never contaminated by Mary but remains fully human because he truly 'took part' but not all, that is, not the deadly blood poison of sin. Normally, there is some mixing or intermingling of the two streams. But Mary and child had two separate blood systems that by a miracle of the Holy Spirit, did not mix or intermingle through her membrane.

The blood of Christ is different from ours because it is 'His own blood' (Rev 1:5). Again, we are told 'the Holy Spirit has purchased the church of God with His own blood' (Act 20:28) so it is also called the blood of God, and the blood of the Holy Spirit!

'Without controversy, great is the mystery...God was manifested in the flesh' (1 Tim 3:16). This 'great mystery' or 'great secret' of the incarnation disappears into the 'blood'.

WHO IS JESUS?

THEY SAID TO HIM, 'Who are You anyway?' Jesus replied, 'Why do I even speak to you!' (Jn 8:25 AMP). 'They still didn't get it, didn't realize He was referring to the Father. So Jesus tried again' (Jn 8:27 MSG), '**When** you have lifted up the Son of Man (on the Cross) **then** you will know that I AM' the Father (Jn 8:28 AMP, Wuest).

'Philip said to Him, Lord, show us the Father - cause us to see the Father, that is all we ask, then we shall be satisfied. Jesus replied, Have I been with all of you for so long a time and you do not recognize and know Me yet, Philip? Anyone who has seen Me has seen the Father. How can you say then, Show us the Father? Do you not believe...the Father is in Me? (Jn 14:8-10 AMP).

Jesus said until He came 'no man has seen God at any time' (Jn 1:18). Christ explains here, what Moses said when the 70 Elders went up on Mount Sinai and 'they saw God' standing on 'as it were, a paved work of sapphire stone, like the very heavens in its clarity' (Ex 24:10).

The Greek word 'seen' is 'horao' (hor-ah-o) which means 'to fully comprehend, perceive the essence of what is seen with the eyes' (Maurice Fuller). This indicates the Elders could not 'fully comprehend' or 'perceive' who they were looking at when 'they saw God' up on the mountain.

Jesus said that was going to change, because 'when you have lifted (Me) up (on the cross) then you will know that I AM' the Father (Jn 8:28 AMP, Wuest). And they did know, because after it was over they were all 'converted' (Lk 27:47,48 Strong).

'**When** the centurion **saw** what happened…and the **whole crowd** who came together to that sight, **seeing** what had been done beat their breasts and **returned** (or) turned quite around, reverse, revolution, **converted**' (Lk 23:47,48 Strong)

'The centurion' and 'the whole crowd' had been filled with furious rage - in a riot condition, screaming 'Away with Him! Away with Him! Crucify Him!' (Jn 19:15 NKJ). But when they 'saw what happened' at the cross they suddenly 'turned around' or 'reversed' themselves, that is, had a personal 'revolution' by repentance and were 'converted'.

Why? Why did His enemies suddenly become believers? What 'happened' to cool their boiling fury? What caused them to 'turn around' and instantly, completely change their hearts and minds? Why will you see all these people in heaven? Their eyes had been opened, and they **knew** Who He was!

Why? What 'happened' to open their eyes? 'The centurion...and all the multitudes **saw** what had taken place...and all His acquaintances who stood at a distance...**saw** these things' (Lk 23:47-49 RSV). **What** did they see?

How could they see when 'darkness came over the whole land' (Lk 23:44 NIV)? What caused it? No eclipse of the sun can last for three hours, so there is no natural explanation. But John tells us the 'king' or 'angel of the bottomless pit...was given the key...he opened (it) and smoke arose out of the pit like the smoke of a great furnace - so the sun and the air were darkened' (Rev 9:11,1,2).

When 'the bottomless pit was opened' millions of these demonic 'rulers of darkness' (Eph 6:12) billowed up into the heavens like great clouds of black smoke blotting out the sun. Any place or coven dedicated by a pact with the Devil, is always dark and gloomy, even though there are many windows and lots of access to the light of day.

This was the thickest, heaviest, darkest concentration of every fallen angel and demon from Hell in the history of the world. What 'happened' at the cross was not unlike 'total darkness (that) covered all the land of Egypt...but all the Israelites had light in the places where they lived' (Ex 10:22,23 NIV).

THE LIGHT OF THE WORLD

JESUS SAID, 'As long as I am in the world, I am the light of the world' (Jn 9:5) and that 'light' could not be turned off while He hung on the cross. Christ was 'transfigured before them. His face shone like the sun' (Mat 17:2) not only in the 'high mountain' but here on Calvary. He and His cross were bathed in transfigured light the whole time. How else could they 'see' what 'happened' in 'total darkness'?

'The Sun of Righteousness' (Mal 4:2) dispelled the darkness so even 'His acquaintances who...stood at a distance **watching** these things' (Lk 23:49) could 'see' what was happening and repented. That's when 'He took away' from **us** and upon **Himself** 'all our sins' (Col 2:13,14 NIV) that 'bruised' or 'crushed' (Isa 53:5 Strong) Him.

Notwithstanding the light and the glory, Jesus was at the same time assaulted by spiritually super-heated 'heaviness' and hopelessness on the cross. If 'the joy of the Lord is our strength' (Neh 8:10) then 'the spirit of heaviness' (Isa 61:3), discouragement and despair is our weakness. 'Heaviness' means 'to be weak' (Strong).

Satan 'bruised His heel' (Gen 3:15) as he and all his forces went on the attack, but then Christ proceeded to 'crush his head'. He tied a chain around the neck of 'that serpent of old, the Devil` and dragged him across the stage of the cosmos (Rev 20:1-3). Now Satan is sitting in a hole, a 'pit' with the most awful headache, wrapped all round with a bandage because his skull has been caved in!

`The hostile princes and rulers He stripped off from Himself and boldly displayed them as His conquests **when, by the cross**, He triumphed over them' (Col 2:15 Wey). He 'stripped off from Himself' the hostile hordes who had wrapped themselves around Him, and then proceeded to '**disarm** powers and authorities...**by the cross**' (Col 2:15 NIV).

'Disarm' is 'to wholly strip off (Thayer), strip arms from a foe' (Vine) - cause to sink out of, put off, take off clothing, unclothe' (Strong). Imagine all those naked 'principalities and powers' reeling backwards from the overwhelming, crushing counter offence of Christ because they no longer had anything to fight with!

SATAN CONQUERED

THE VEIL WAS DRAWN back for us when 'He made a public spectacle, exhibit, example of **them**, triumphing over **them**' (Col 2:15 NIV, Strong, Thayer) that is, the whole demonic world. 'Triumph' is a big, strong word with combined cognates that mean 'the triumphant display of the defeated (Vine), to conquer, give victory, frighten to a noisy wail, clamor, to light, kindle, set on fire' (Strong).

Christ not only frightened 'them' into total chaos confusion and disarray, but 'set on fire' the whole demonic world! Satan and 'all the multitudes' (Lk 23:48,49 RSV) around the cross, watched his 'kingdom of darkness' exploding and collapsing all around him because all this was 'made public' and they 'saw these things'. No wonder everyone repented! So would you, and so would I…

'For this the Son of God was manifested that He might **destroy, dismiss, dissolve, demolish, deprive of authority, do away with** the works of the Devil' (1 Jn 3:8 Thayer). The glue that held the 'works of the Devil' together was 'dissolved' and it all fell apart like rotten ice!

The cross provided the legal basis for the Kingdom of Christ to enforce His conquest of the Kingdom of Satan. As a result, `you are complete **in Him**, who is the head of **all** principality and power` (Col 2:10). The 'man, Christ Jesus' (1 Tim 2:5) is now the head of Satan himself and all 'principalities, powers, rulers of the darkness of this world and spiritual hosts of wickedness' (Eph 6:12). 'He is Lord of **all**' (Act 10:36) that is, Lord of **all** holy and unholy angels and **all** the 'great multitude which no man can number' (Rev 7:9).

'God was not **imputing** their trespasses to them…for He made Him to **be** sin for us, who **knew** no sin, that we might be made the righteousness of God in Him' (2 Cor 5:19,21). The context indicates Jesus became the sin-center of the world because it was 'imputed' legally, not imparted experientially.

THE SECOND EXODUS

⁂

WHEN 'MOSES and Elijah appeared in glory and spoke of His **decease** or 'exodus' which He should accomplish at Jerusalem' (Lk 9:31) they were talking about His 'exit' or moving out. They said it's time to move out! There is a way out of the chaos, confusion and disorder in this world - also that thousands of people in Paradise are all excited about your coming!

We were told to come and tell you they're all waiting for you down there. Isaiah said he wrote about this day and now it's coming to pass! Abraham said he 'rejoiced' or 'jumped for joy' (Jn 8:56 Strong) to see this day 2000 years ago, and it's even greater than he thought. They both wanted to come but we were appointed. Everyone is all stirred up down there - so why all the excitement?

They knew 'the strategic time for fulfillment is now at hand' (Rev 1:3 Weymouth, Wuest). Every time an Israelite sacrificed an animal in his own place, it was a promissory note to be paid by the blood of Christ on this great day of redemption.

When Jesus died 'He first **descended** into the lower Hades, parts, section of the universe' (Eph 4:9 Strong, Thayer) but His entrance into Paradise was not easily gained. Satan's vigilance knew no bounds. He had been standing on 'guard' for thousands of years.

As Christ the King approached this 'prison' or 'isolation ward' (1 Pet 3:19 Strong) behind the 'everlasting doors' the great crowd of believers on the other side cried 'Lift up your heads, O gates! Be lifted up, you everlasting doors! And the King of glory shall come in' (Psa 24:7).

Satan the 'sentinel' (Thayer) hurled back the challenge '**Who is,** this King of glory?' (Psa 24:8). The crowd replied 'the Lord strong and mighty. The Lord mighty in battle'. He's coming from the battle fields of Golgotha where He single-handedly defeated and 'destroyed' you and your 'power of death' (Heb 2:14).

Now 'lift up your heads, O gates! Lift up, you everlasting doors! And the King of glory shall come in'. Still unconvinced and unsatisfied, Satan's challenge rang out '**Who is He** then, (NBV) this King of glory?' This time the crowd roars '**The Lord of hosts, He** is the King of glory' (Psa 24:9,10).

When Satan saw the the smoking ruins of his kingdom and knew he and his whole demonic world had been defeated and destroyed 'by the cross' (Col 2:15) and by fire - he had to give up. The 'gates of Hades' (Mat 16:18) and the 'everlasting doors' could prevail no longer. They **had** to be '**lifted up**' and have never been let down. Those 'gates' and 'doors' are still open.

THE KEYS OF HELL

WHEN CHRIST the King came in, He confronted Satan by saying, I'll take those keys! Satan said, No one ever talked to me like this before. Jesus said, No one ever had the authority or legal right, to do so before. The Son of God 'dismissed' Satan (1 Jn 3:8) and the 'keys' **had** to be handed over. Jesus said Now 'I have the keys of Hades and Death' (Rev 1:18).

We have been taught to sing 'He tore the bars away' and 'up from the grave He arose' but Christ did not tear the bars away. Jesus rested and rejoiced with Moses, Elijah and all the saints in Paradise for three full days and nights, then put the 'key' in the lock, opened the door and said Come on! Let's go! Satan no longer had the authority to stop them.

Then began another great triumphal procession as they started up the stairs of the Ascension. 'When He **ascended** on high He led captivity captive...**far above all the heavens**' (Eph 4:8,10). But when they got to Jerusalem on the way up, some of the saints said Do you mind if we stop-over? We haven't seen the old hometown for centuries.

Then 'the graves were opened and **many** bodies of the saints who had fallen asleep were raised out of the graves after His resurrection, they went into the holy city and **appeared to many**' (Mat 27:52,53). Up from their graves they arose!

Jesus wasn't the only one who rose from the dead! He brought a lot of others with Him. This time it wasn't just Moses and Elijah. Now 'many saints' including Abraham and Isaiah were there. **They** '**appeared** to many' too, not just Peter, James and John who were with Jesus in the mountain.

What an amazing surprise and experience it must have been for Abraham to walk up to Mary and say Hi, how are you doing? You know, I understand some of what you went through when I laid Isaac on the altar. I saw it all coming. Imagine the conversations people had with the elders of old!

Then Jesus led them up the last flight of stairs in the Ascension and David's prophetic word came to pass: 'Though You lie down among the sheepfolds You will be like the wings of a dove covered with silver, and her feathers with yellow gold...You have ascended on high - You have led captivity captive and received gifts for men' (Psa 68:13,18).

Although Christ laid Himself down 'among the sheepfolds' like a Lamb for the slaughter, He arose 'like a Dove' who shook off the soot and dirt of chimney smoke that fills a polluted world, into the sunshine and bright white light of a New Day. The golden glory and redemptive silver that covered His wings, lifted Him up 'on high'.

THE THRONE OF GOD

❧

PETER SAID on the Day of Pentecost, 'Let me freely speak to you of the patriarch David...that God had sworn He would raise up Christ to sit on his throne (Psa 132:1) he spoke concerning the resurrection of Christ' (Act 2:29-31). This means the Pentecostal outpouring is connected to and related to David.

After the ascension of Christ, what **descended** at Pentecost was Coronation Oil being poured out on the head of David's Son who was now crowned God's New King. Every time the Holy Spirit is poured out upon us '**we see** Him crowned' in a fresh, new revelation of His 'glory and honor' (Heb 2:9). Pentecost is much more than a bit of blessing or a few frothy bubbles of 'new wine'. Pentecost is an outpouring of spiritual authority!

This 'holy anointing oil' (Ex 30:25) came pouring down, not only on Christ the Head but upon 'the church which is His body' (Eph 1:22,23) - just as the 'precious oil' came 'running down on the beard of Aaron, to the edge of his garments' (Psa 133:2). This 'precious oil' came down to fill and baptize God's 'Royal Priesthood' (1 Pet 2:9) with kingly authority in the Divine Coronation of 'kings and priests unto God' (Rev 1:6).

When 'the apostles asked Lord, will You at this time restore the Kingdom?' (Act 1:1,6) His answer was 'It is not for you to know the times or seasons' (Act 1:7) but **yes**. I will restore the Kingdom! 'You shall receive **power** after that the Holy Spirit has come upon you' (Act 1:8).

When Pentecost came 'tongues of fire **sat** (kathizo) upon each one' (Act 2:3). This word 'sat' means 'to confer the Kingdom upon one' (Thayer) so the Kingdom came to each one of them personally, but not in the way they expected. The same word is used when Christ was 'raised up to **sit** on his throne' (Act 2:30). God conferred the Kingdom on both Christ and His apostles at that 'time'.

After His resurrection and ascension 'the **Man**, Christ Jesus' (1 Tim 2:5) stepped up to the Throne of **God** and presented His tokens of redemption – millions of them! And God said Sit down Son, and reign, until you complete your conquest. You conquered the Devil and destroyed his 'works of darkness' - now conquer the world, and hand it back to Me finished.

'Then comes **The End** when 'the Man' delivers the kingdom to God the Father...for 'the **Man**' must reign till He has put all enemies under His feet. The last enemy that will be destroyed is death' (1 Cor 15:24-26). God chose one of us - we who spend all our lifetime in 'earthen vessels' (2 Cor 4:7) made of mud. He chose One who is truly a 'Man' not an angel.

This 'Man' now sits on the throne of God in the place of 'power and authority' over the ever expanding universe. Of the increase of His government and peace there will be no end. (Isaiah 9:7). The astounding magnitude of this reality is overwhelming and awesome beyond words!

DIMENSIONS OF THE CROSS

By the Rev G A Batke
1903 - 1964

HAVE you ever thought of it? Pondered it well? For never can the remembrance of Christ, staggering uphill with a huge wooden cross beam under a blazing Judean sun become obliterated from the mind of the historian or heart of God's dear children. The cross...the crucifixion.

Remember the shiny rippling of muscles up and down the powerful arm of a Roman soldier as he was driving heavy spikes through the quivering flesh of Christ, and the uplifting of His body high into the air. Remember the revulsion of outraged nerves, pain that shot like jagged daggers through that blessed body - and His words, 'This is my body which is broken for you'.

There were the hours of insufferable pain and anguish of spirit, the hot sun beating down on His uncovered head (except the thorns), flies and ants feeding on the clotted blood of open wounds, mixed with human spittle drying on His face. While angels wept, earth and rocks convulsed, and all the demons of hell billowed up like black smoke until the sun was blotted out, the earth darkened.

But greater still, His heart! Bearing human misunderstanding alienation and cruelty, then on the cross the sins of the whole world. Not self-pity or just physical suffering, but the crushing load of our sin and full fury that fell on Him Who hung in our place until even the wrath of God was exhausted! All this broke the heart of Jesus.

Let us, for a few moments calculate the dimensions of the cross: its height, then its depth, its length and then its breadth. Oh, I know the actual dimensions would not be so difficult to guess, but the spiritual dimensions - who can circumvent their scope? Calculate them in the light of the 'determinate counsel and foreknowledge of God'.

He measures the cross with the yardstick of eternity. 'Slain' says God, 'from the foundation of the world'. Again, 'Christ died for the sins of the whole world' and again, 'Christ died for the ungodly'. 'Wherefore' says God, 'He is able to save them to the uttermost that come unto God by Him'. Who can measure the scope of such mighty dimensions, except God Himself?

Can you measure the height of the cross? So high that its summit reached up to heaven where the Plan and Person of the cross originated. It was the mind of God that planned redemption by blood, it was the heart of God which 'so loved the world that He gave'.... No higher source of man's redemption can be found than the up reach of the cross.

Can you fathom the depth of the cross? How far down did its stem reach? Deep down into the earth its base was plunged, deeper still its spiritual depth. The depth of the cross went down to 'where we were'. Down to where the dwellers of everlasting night living out their living death, waiting to be engulfed by the 'second death'. Yes, down to the depths of Hell itself. And when the cross dropped into that hole in Calvary, the 'lowest hell' shook, and through its virtue sinners of the deepest hue come forth, not to die but to live!

Can you measure the length of the cross? Ages upon ages have heard of His 'longsuffering'. Resounding echoes have girdled the world again and again. All races, all creeds, all kinds, the good and the bad, from generation to generation have heard and lived. Who can describe its mighty outreach to all men of all ages? Glory to God!

Can you span the breadth of the cross? And here our thoughts are awed with the immensity of it all. For from sinner to saint, from hell to heaven, from death to life, from Satan to God, from the uttermost to the uttermost, its exceedingly broad beam spanned the gulf - and man walked into the arms of God!

The breadth of the cross will only be appreciated when glory itself, age to age will unfold its mysteries. Salvation through 'the blood of His cross', baptism in the Holy Spirit - healing and other gifts of the Spirit, are all virtues drawn from its sacred stem, and still there is more than enough to spare.

ROOM AT THE CROSS.

There is room at the cross, Let us take shelter.

I, Lionel C Batke, do not claim to fully comprehend all Divine **revelation** at this time. The work of the Holy Spirit is to **progressively** lead and guide God's people into all truth, through **illumination** of the heart and mind. Since all creeds are merely human attempts to systematically express absolute and eternal truth, they are at best, but fallible philosophy.

Traditional terms and labels have, without exception, proven to be profoundly false guides! Far more truth has been lost than saved by trying to conveniently compress a whole doctrine, or the sum of all Scriptures on a given subject, into one or two extra-biblical words. Many implications followed through to their logical conclusion, deepen into tremendous travesty that finally fabricates and falsifies the truth.

In order to restore and retain a clear vision of the whole truth once and for all delivered to the saints, it is essential to obey the voice of the Holy Spirit, and wholeheartedly love the God of all truth. As the truth of God comes into highly defined focus once more - healthy and accurate doctrinal thinking can be achieved. With overflowing heart therefore, I accept affirm and believe in:

1) The full and complete, word by word inspiration of the Bible or accepted canon of Holy Scriptures, which are thus infallibly true and correct in their consensus of original manuscripts and therefore, the supreme and final authority in all matters of faith and practice.

2) The autonomous existence and distinctive self-revelation of one and only one, true and living God, Creator of heaven and earth, who has fully expressed and manifested Himself as God the Father in the Son by the power of the Holy Spirit, in order to inter-act with a fallen world and reconcile sinful man.

3) The creation, test and fall of man as recorded in Genesis, his total spiritual depravity and inability to attain Divine righteousness by human effort.

4) The eternal Deity of Jesus Christ including His preexistence as Jehovah the Most High and Almighty God, whose human nature was conceived by a miracle of the Holy Spirit, born of the virgin Mary, made both Lord and Christ and therefore, the only begotten Son and Savior of men – very God and very man!

5) That same Jesus, how that He died on the cross for the remission of our sins while remaining holy and separate from sinners, was buried, then rose again the third day for our justification before God.

6) The Gospel of Grace, namely, the salvation of sinners by grace alone through faith in the perfect, sufficient sacrifice and finished work of Christ on the cross.

7) The Gospel of the Kingdom, how that Jesus bodily ascended to Heaven and was seated as a man on the throne of God from which he now rules and reigns - and will personally return to translate His Church at the

second coming of Christ, commonly called the end of the world or dissolution of the universe.

8) The eternal, invisible Kingdom of God including the Kingdom of his Son, in present power and reality, which began with His resurrection and is growing throughout the Gospel and Church age to its completion and full manifestation in the new heavens and the new earth.

9) Believer's baptism by immersion in water in the Name of the Lord Jesus Christ, as an expression of true Christian faith, and as an act of obedience that fulfills His command.

10) Baptism in the Holy Spirit for believers as an experience subsequent to salvation, accompanied by the initial, physical evidence of speaking in tongues as the Spirit gives utterance, and other scriptural signs that follow.

11) The full release and free exercise of all Spiritual Gifts by believers today according to the Scriptures, and as manifested in the early Church.

12) The contemporary healing of spirit, soul and body by Divine power, or Divine healing in its many aspects as taught in Holy Scripture and practiced by the early church.

13) The Spirit filled life of separation from the world and perfecting of holiness by renewing the mind in the fear of God, as an expression of true transformation.

14) The eternal life of the believer and everlasting damnation of the unbeliever, in eternal fire.

15) The Church holy, apostolic, universal and indivisible.

16) The autonomy of the local church, led by its elders in oversight, and interdependent fellowship with other churches, especially in the same area, as an expression of unity in the Holy Spirit.

17) The multiple ministries of apostles, prophets, evangelists, pastors and teachers, all of which are essential in equipping and preparing saints for the work of the ministry.

18) The Lord's Supper as an ordinance for believers through which we partake by faith, of the spiritual presence of Christ, and acknowledge our communion in the church, which is His body, remembering His death and coming again.

19) The reality, personality, and ministry of holy angels.

20) The reality and personality of demons, fallen angels and Satan, adversary of God and enemy of the Church – how that Christ crushed his head, conquered him at Calvary and sealed his doom.

NOTES

PROLOGUE

1. Proverbs 25:11 (NKJV)
2. Proverbs25:11 (NET Bible)
3. Matthew 13:52 (Contemporary English Version)

1. GOD HAS SPOKEN!

1. Hebrews 1:1-2

2. REGENERATION

1. (1 Cor 2:11,14 Amp)

3. HERMEN WHO?

1. Joseph Henry Thayer's Greek–English Lexicon of the New Testament
2. Kittel, Gerhard; Friedrich, Gerhard. *Theological Dictionary of the New Testament, 10 Volumes.* 10 Vols. Eerdmans, 1977.
3. Strongest Strong's Exhaustive Concordance of the Bible

19. DUST AND DEITY

1. The New Testament: An Expanded Translation, by Kenneth S Wuest.

Printed in France by Amazon
Brétigny-sur-Orge, FR